my revis

EDEXCEL A2
ECONOMICS

Quintin Brewer
Rachel Cole

Hodder Education, an Hachette UK company, 338 Euston Road, London NW1 3BH

Orders
Bookpoint Ltd, 130 Milton Park, Abingdon, Oxfordshire OX14 4SB
tel: 01235 827827
fax: 01235 400401
e-mail: education@bookpoint.co.uk
Lines are open 9.00 a.m.–5.00 p.m., Monday to Saturday, with a 24-hour message answering service. You can also order through the Hodder Education website: www.hoddereducation.co.uk

ISBN 978-1-4441-7982-8

First printed 2013
Impression number 5 4 3 2 1
Year 2017 2016 2015 2014 2013

Cover photo reproduced by permission of hs-creator/Fotolia

Typeset by Datapage (India) Pvt. Ltd.
Printed in India

Hachette UK's policy is to use papers that are natural, renewable and recyclable products and made from wood grown in sustainable forests. The logging and manufacturing processes are expected to conform to the environmental regulations of the country of origin.

P2185

Get the most from this book

Everyone has to decide his or her own revision strategy, but it is essential to review your work, learn it and test your understanding. These Revision Notes will help you to do that in a planned way, topic by topic. Use this book as the cornerstone of your revision and don't hesitate to write in it — personalise your notes and check your progress by ticking off each section as you revise.

Tick to track your progress

Use the revision planner on pages 4 and 5 to plan your revision, topic by topic. Tick each box when you have:

- revised and understood a topic
- tested yourself
- practised the exam questions and gone online to check your answers and complete the quick quizzes

You can also keep track of your revision by ticking off each topic heading in the book. You may find it helpful to add your own notes as you work through each topic.

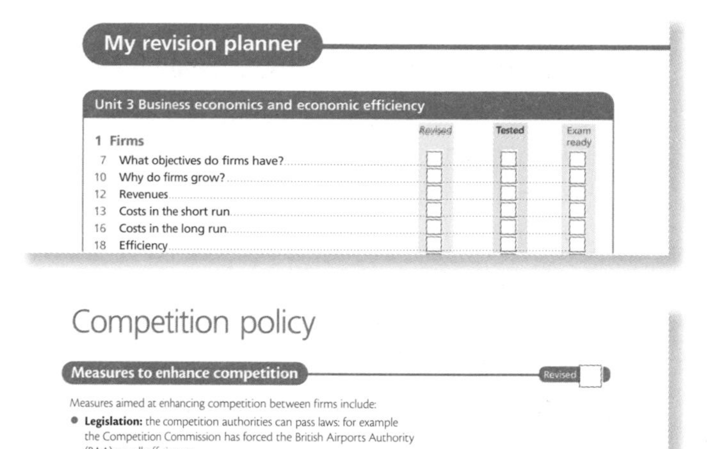

Features to help you succeed

Examiner's tips and summaries

Expert tips are given throughout the book to help you polish your exam technique in order to maximise your chances. The summaries provide a quick-check bullet list for each topic.

Typical mistakes

The authors identify the typical mistakes candidates make and explain how you can avoid them.

Now test yourself

These short, knowledge-based questions provide the first step in testing your learning. Answers are at the back of the book.

Definitions and key words

Clear, concise definitions of essential key terms are provided on the page where they appear.

Key words from the specification are highlighted in bold for you throughout the book.

Revision activities

These activities will help you to understand each topic in an interactive way.

Exam practice

Practice exam questions are provided for each topic. Use them to consolidate your revision and practise your exam skills.

Online

Go online to check your answers to the exam questions and try out the extra quick quizzes at **www.therevisionbutton.co.uk/myrevisionnotes**

My revision planner

Unit 3 Business economics and economic efficiency

Unit 4 The global economy

Revised | Tested | Exam ready

Exam practice answers and quick quizzes at www.therevisionbutton.co.uk/myrevisionnotes

Countdown to my exams

6–8 weeks to go

- Start by looking at the specification — make sure you know exactly what material you need to revise and the style of the examination. Use the revision planner on pages 4 and 5 to familiarise yourself with the topics.
- Organise your notes, making sure you have covered everything on the specification. The revision planner will help you to group your notes into topics.
- Work out a realistic revision plan that will allow you time for relaxation. Set aside days and times for all the subjects that you need to study, and stick to your timetable.
- Set yourself sensible targets. Break your revision down into focused sessions of around 40 minutes, divided by breaks. These Revision Notes organise the basic facts into short, memorable sections to make revising easier.

Revised ☐

4–6 weeks to go

- Read through the relevant sections of this book and refer to the examiner's tips, examiner's summaries, typical mistakes and key terms. Tick off the topics as you feel confident about them. Highlight those topics you find difficult and look at them again in detail.
- Test your understanding of each topic by working through the 'Now test yourself' questions and 'Revision activities' in the book. Look up the answers at the back of the book.
- Make a note of any problem areas as you revise, and ask your teacher to go over these in class.
- Look at past papers. They are one of the best ways to revise and practise your exam skills. Write or prepare planned answers to the exam practice questions provided in this book. Check your answers online and try out the extra quick quizzes at **www.therevisionbutton.co.uk/myrevisionnotes**
- Use the revision activities to try different revision methods. For example, you can make notes using mind maps, spider diagrams or flash cards.
- Track your progress using the revision planner and give yourself a reward when you have achieved your target.

Revised ☐

One week to go

- Try to fit in at least one more timed practice of an entire past paper and seek feedback from your teacher, comparing your work closely with the mark scheme.
- Check the revision planner to make sure you haven't missed out any topics. Brush up on any areas of difficulty by talking them over with a friend or getting help from your teacher.
- Attend any revision classes put on by your teacher. Remember, he or she is an expert at preparing people for examinations.

Revised ☐

The day before the examination

- Flick through these Revision Notes for useful reminders, for example the examiner's tips, examiner's summaries, typical mistakes and key terms.
- Check the time and place of your examination.
- Make sure you have everything you need — extra pens and pencils, tissues, a watch, bottled water, sweets.
- Allow some time to relax and have an early night to ensure you are fresh and alert for the examinations.

Revised ☐

My exams

A2 Economics Unit 3

Date: ....

Time: ....

Location: ....

A2 Economics Unit 4

Date: ....

Time: ....

Location: ....

1 Firms

A **firm** is a production unit. Its function is to transform factors of production such as raw materials and workers into goods and services.

A firm can exist in the **private sector** — meaning that individuals, not the government, own the firm; or it could be owned by the government, that is the **public sector**, for example some dentists and other health workers, the London underground and the post office.

A **firm** is a production unit.

The **private sector** involves assets owned by individuals or groups, not the government. An example is a Bupa hospital. It is funded by private payments from individuals or companies.

The **public sector** involves assets owned by society as a whole, provided through the government. An example is an NHS hospital. It is funded mainly through taxation.

What objectives do firms have?

The objective of the firm will depend on whether it is in the private or public sector.

- **Private sector** firms have to make a profit to survive, so to some extent making a profit has to be a primary objective of firms in the private sector. Whether private sector firms aim to *maximise* profit is something we are going to discuss below.
- **Public sector** firms, however, can survive without making a profit because the government can make up any shortfall in revenues. But some public sector firms aim to make a profit, for example the Royal Mail, although it may have other aims which are more important. For the Royal Mail this may be the quality of service, or the fact that it undertakes to deliver to everyone in the country regardless of where they live — the 'universal' service. Another example is the BBC, which is publicly owned and its primary aim is to entertain and educate. If public sector firms do not make a profit, they have to compromise some of their other objectives. For instance, the BBC has had to cut back the range of programming to reduce costs. If public sector firms do not have any ambition to make a profit, they will soon become inefficient and loss-making, which itself compromises the firm's main objectives.

We are going to look at private sector firms for the majority of this book, returning to public sector enterprises and their efficiency in Chapter 3 (pages 37–40).

Profit maximisation

Revised

While all firms in the private sector have to make a profit in order to survive, not all firms maximise profit.

Profit maximisation can be looked at in two ways. Either:

- the total revenue and total cost are at their greatest difference apart; or price take away cost per unit, multiplied by quantity, is greatest

Examiner's tip

Profit maximisation is the assumption for private sector firms and you should assume this is the aim of a firm unless you are told otherwise.

- or the point where the revenue gained from selling one more unit (**marginal revenue**, MR) is exactly equal to the cost of producing one more unit (**marginal cost**, MC). In shorthand this is written as MR = MC

It means that the firm is making most money relative to the costs. Often, this means that the firm is not making the most amount of *revenue* possible. This is in fact a different objective called revenue maximisation (see below).

We say that profit maximisation is rational or properly reasoned: if there is an opportunity for a firm to make more profit we assume this is better for the firm than to make less profit. Profit is the reward for risk-taking, so it is rational that the risk-taker will want to get the greatest reward possible.

Looking at MR = MC, if a firm sells one more unit and gets more money coming in than it costs to make that unit, then it is rational for the firm to produce and sell that unit. We say that the **marginal profit** is positive. By contrast, if in selling another unit the costs are *greater* than the revenue received, we say the marginal profit is *negative* and the firm would be advised to reduce output. When the marginal cost equals the marginal revenue the firm reaches equilibrium — or balanced state — meaning there is no tendency either to increase or decrease output, because either of those options would reduce the profitability of the firm.

Marginal revenue (MR) is the change in revenue from selling one more unit of output. If price is constant then price = marginal revenue. But if price has to be lowered to sell more, then marginal revenue falls (it has twice the gradient of the demand curve). Marginal revenue can be positive or negative. When marginal revenue is positive the demand curve is relatively price elastic. When marginal revenue is negative the demand curve is relatively price inelastic. Marginal revenue is the gradient of the total revenue curve.

Marginal cost (MC) is the extra cost of making one more unit of output. Marginal cost is always positive. The marginal cost curve always rises in the short run, as soon as the law of diminishing returns sets in. MC is the gradient of the total cost curve.

Marginal profit is the extra profit gained from selling one more unit. When marginal profit is zero, the firm is maximising profit. Marginal profit = MR – MC.

Now test yourself Tested

1 Is profit maximisation an equilibrium point? Do I assume all firms are profit maximisers?

Answers on p. 109

Revenue maximisation

Revised

If you ignored all the costs of a firm, or if there are no variable costs, then an alternative to profit maximisation might be that the firm aims to maximise its revenue. This means it cuts its price down to the point where the extra revenue received from selling another unit is balanced by the reduced price on every item it is already selling. We say marginal revenue is zero, or MR = 0.

If marginal cost is zero — i.e. there are no variable costs — that is the same as profit maximisation because if MR = 0 and MC = 0, then MR = MC. However, this is not very likely and therefore revenue maximisation is not fully rational. Firms are making as much money as they can but ignoring the fact that, on some units, costs are greater than the revenue they are receiving so it would be better to cut down on production.

There are some circumstances, however, that would make revenue maximisation a reasonable choice:

- If a firm is going to have to dispose of all its stock, then effectively the costs are not relevant. For example, a flower-seller who has bought the stock in the morning, and cannot sell it the next day because the flowers will have wilted, is logical in maximising revenue.

- If a business is owned and managed by different people, there might be different objectives. The owners might be the shareholders who will want maximum profit, but the managers — that is, the people making the decisions about how much to produce — might be paid according to how much is made or sold, for example through performance-related pay or bonuses based on turnover (revenue). In this case, it would be logical for the managers of the firm to maximise revenue.
- If a firm is about to be taken over by another firm it may be valued on the basis of its revenue. So firms might try to maximise their revenue to ensure that the sale price is as high as possible.

Now test yourself Tested

2 At the end of a day's trading, a flower seller cuts prices of all the stock that will not last until the following day. What pricing strategy is this?

Answers on p. 109

Sales maximisation

Revised

This occurs when a firm *sells as much as possible* subject to the constraint that it *at least makes normal profit* (see page 14). The firm might increase market share and get rid of competitors by cutting its price. This might be a short-run policy and in the long run the firm might want to return to profit maximisation. This can be shown on a diagram (see Figure 1.1):

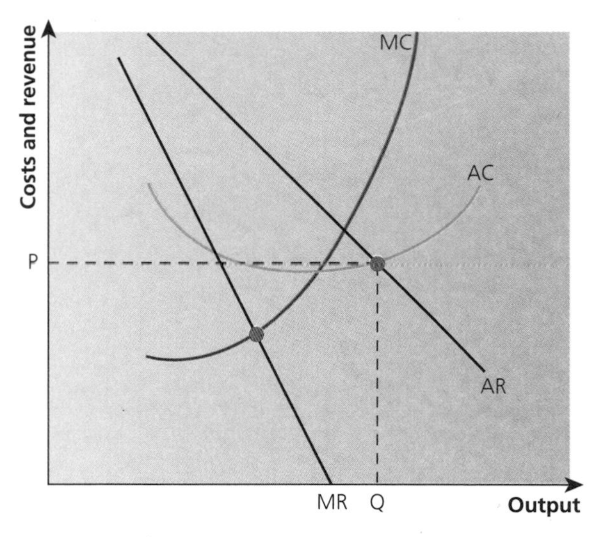

Figure 1.1 Sales maximisation occurs at Q where AC = AR

One reason for sales maximisation is to avoid the attention of the competition authorities. The government is often involved as a watchdog for private firms and if firms are seen to be making a large amount of profit they may be subject to investigation.

Another reason for sales maximisation is that a high level of profitability might attract other firms into the market, so by cutting prices and selling more, new entry is prevented.

Typical mistake

Do not confuse sales maximisation with sales revenue maximisation. The latter is just another name for revenue maximisation (MR = 0) and ignores costs.

Now test yourself Tested

3 Do sales-maximising firms have lower or higher prices than profit-maximising firms?

Answers on p. 109

Examiner's tip

Sales maximisation is also sometimes called output maximisation. It means making as much output as possible subject to the condition of not making a loss.

Behavioural theories

Revised

While it is nice to draw a neat picture using the assumption that firms behave in a rational way, firms' objectives do not always seem to be rational. The human intentions and the interaction of the people that run the firms can have a significant impact on output and pricing decisions. The characteristics of the owner or manager will be reflected in the objectives of the firm. For example:

- If a person wants to run a business with low risk, the business might be kept small, producing just enough to make a certain amount of profit that will pay the costs.
- Firms may wish to keep profits down to avoid being taken over by other firms, and the managers might get some satisfaction from being in control of their own business which is worth more than money.
- Some firms will aim to make just enough profit to keep the shareholders happy and then pursue other objectives. For example, a manager may choose to go and play golf rather than sell a few more items because he knows he has reached his sales targets and making any more money will not be as much fun. This policy of *satisfying* the shareholders with *sufficient* profit is described by an economics term you need to know: **satisficing**.

Satisficing is where a firm aims to make sufficient profit to satisfy the shareholders, leaving it free then to pursue other aims.

As with the objectives above, apart from profit maximisation, we assume there is a divorce or disconnect between the owners and the managers of a firm.

Now test yourself Tested

4 Why do some firms engage in satisficing?

Answers on p. 109

Why do firms grow?

The reasons why a firm grows will primarily depend on its objectives. If a firm wants to *profit maximise* it may need to grow larger in order to make all the profit that is available. If a firm is *sales* or *revenue maximising* it will want to grow, subject to certain constraints as discussed above on pages 8–9 Firms may wish to grow because the status of a manager will improve or because workers' motivation is driven by performance-related pay or because the bigger the firm is, the more people will get paid.

Benefits of growth

Revised

What are the benefits of growth to a firm?

- **Economies of scale:** larger firms often have lower costs per unit of output in the long run. These are discussed in more detail on page 16.
- **Increased market share:** a larger firm has more market power, can control prices and retain consumer loyalty. A larger market share also means that the threat of competitors is reduced.
- **Economies of scope:** larger firms are less exposed to the risk that firms might have if they are narrowly focused; especially in times of recession, the dangers of being too uniquely focused can cause uncertainty for a firm's future.
- **Psychological factors:** managers may gain more job satisfaction from working for a well-known brand and having responsibility for large numbers of people. The larger the firm, the bigger its profile tends to be.

Economies of scale occur when an increase in the scale of production results in a fall in long-run average costs.

How do firms grow?

Revised

There are three main ways a firm can grow:

- **Horizontal integration:** this is when firms merge at the same stage of the same production process. The firms may not make exactly the same product, and are likely to want to increase the range of products they produce, or are keen to get into new markets around the world.

  For example, when Kraft bought Cadbury in 2010 for £11.9 billion Kraft already made some chocolate products (Terry's chocolate, Oreo chocolate biscuits and Milka chocolate) so they acquired new brands such as Cadbury's Creme Egg, but more importantly they gained access to large parts of the European chocolate market.
- **Vertical integration:** this is when firms merge at different stages of the production process. This can be broken down into two further types. Backward vertical integration means that one firm is buying another firm that is closer to the raw material stage of production. For example, if a steel maker buys a coal-producing firm, this is backward vertical integration because steel production uses a lot of coal.

  Forward vertical integration means buying another firm in the same production process but closer to the customer. For example, a brewery buying a chain of pubs engages in forward vertical integration.
- **Conglomerate integration or diversification:** this is sometimes also called lateral integration. It occurs when a firm buys another firm in a completely unrelated business. A commonly used example is Virgin, a company owned by Richard Branson, that buys anything from trains and aeroplanes to cable internet providers.

Now test yourself

Tested

5 Penguin books has been bought by the German owners of another large publishing company, Random House. What might be the advantages of this merger?

Answers on p. 109

Revision activity

Draw a sketch of a firm that makes something that interests you. Then show all the ways it can integrate, drawing an upwards arrow for backward vertical, downwards arrow for forward vertical etc.

Why do some firms remain small?

Revised

- **Niche market:** some firms operate in very small corners or sections of a market because the demand for the product is specialised and limited.
- **Lack of economies of scale, or existence of diseconomies of scale:** we sometimes say that the firm has a small **minimum efficient scale.** This is the smallest output at which a firm can operate having exploited internal economies of scale. Doctors and dentists usually operate in a small firm owned by 'partners', the practitioners themselves, who can only operate a certain caseload based on the hours of the working week.
- **Need for a dynamic, responsive, service-led firm:** firms involved in design are often small and quick to respond to the needs of larger firms who buy in their services.
- **Heavy government regulation:** some firms are kept small because the government wants to prevent monopolies developing. This is especially true of commercial banks in the US, see Figure 1.6 on page 23.

A **niche market** is a specialised, sub-section of a market which has a unique demand curve and in which there are potential profits to be made.

The **minimum efficient scale** is the smallest output possible at which a firm can operate while experiencing its lowest long-run average costs.

Now test yourself

Tested

6 Morgan Motor Company in Malvern produces less than 700 cars a year and has a long waiting list. List the factors that might explain why this successful company remains small.

Answers on p. 109

Revenues

Total revenue and marginal revenue

Revised

Revenue is the amount of money a firm receives. If everybody pays the same price, the formula is: price multiplied by quantity, P × Q. For example, if I sell 200 doughnuts for 50p each, my total revenue is £100. When we plot the total revenue curve we must consider whether the firm is a price taker, or a **price maker**.

If the firm is a **price taker** it is operating in a very competitive market, and it has to offer its product at the same price as everyone else. If it charges a higher price it will not be able to sell anything.

If the firm cuts the price, it has no advantages because a price taker can sell everything it has at the going rate. A typical example is a fishing boat captain who brings his catch into port in the mornings. The price he gets for his fish will depend entirely on the **demand** and **supply** for that type of fish at that particular port and that time and the fisherman has to accept the price offered. When we draw total revenue for a price taker we will draw a straight line going through the origin. (On page 24 there is a table of all the definitions, formulae, and diagrams you will need.)

However for most firms, the demand curve is downward sloping.

A **price maker** is a firm with such a powerful position in the market that it can set prices.

A **price taker** has to offer its product at the same price as everyone else.

Demand is also known as average revenue.

Supply is the amount which firms are willing to sell at any given price.

When we draw total revenue for a price-making firm, the curve is a **parabola** shape. What this means is that as the price falls the revenue will rise, but it rises more slowly each time that price is cut, up to the point of **maximum revenue**. Eventually it reaches the point where revenue will not increase any more. We say the marginal revenue is zero, that is, MR = 0. Marginal revenue is the increase in revenue when one more unit is sold.

You will realise that **marginal revenue** is less than average revenue — or the price that people are prepared to pay — because when price is cut the firm loses money on all the items it is already selling. Where MR = 0, the amount the firm gets from selling one more item is exactly equal to the amount lost by cutting the price on all the items already being sold. So for example, I am a price-making firm on the beach selling ice creams and I have set the price at £2 per ice cream. I find I cannot sell very many — say 20. My total revenue is £40. I cut the price to increase my sales to £1 and I sell an extra 20 ice creams. My marginal revenue is £20 from selling 20 extra ice creams, but I lose £20 on the ice creams I could have sold at £20 each. My total revenue is still £40; my marginal revenue is zero. The only difference is that I have to sell more ice cream which in fact will cost me more, so I am actually making less profit.

For a price-taking firm, once the total revenue (TR) has reached a maximum, you will then find that TR starts to fall as you cut the prices. It would be stupid for any firm to operate where TR is falling. It means that by selling another item, the gain is actually negative. We call this **relatively inelastic demand**. When you cut the price, you make less money.

A **parabola** shape is an upside-down 'U', in this context.

Revenue maximisation is where the firm makes as much money as it can.

Typical mistake

You might think it is not true that firms will not be able to sell their goods if they charge a higher price. For instance, you might think a corner shop will charge more than the going rate for some items. The answer to this is that the corner shop is not a price taker. It in fact has some monopoly power over its local market. Monopoly power means that it has control over supply and to some extent the firm can set prices and is therefore a price maker.

Average revenue

Revised

Average revenue is the price the firm receives per unit sold. An average revenue curve is the same as the demand curve, or price. Just as with total revenue you can have a price taker and a price maker:

- For average revenue, a price taker has a horizontal demand curve which is perfectly elastic.
- A price maker has a downward sloping demand curve and we draw marginal revenue on the same graph with a gradient twice as steep. As with total revenue, marginal revenue is the amount received for selling one more unit; it is less than average revenue because cutting prices means losing money on items already sold.

Now test yourself

Tested

7 If demand for a product you sell is relatively price inelastic, what should you do?

Answers on p. 109

Costs in the short run

Costs are the payments that firms must make in recompense for use of the factors of production. Rent must be paid for the use of land, wages for the use of labour, and an amount we call interest must be allowed for the use of capital goods. Included in costs is a reward for risk-taking which is known as **normal profit** and this represents the amount the risk-taker must receive to keep resources in their current use. Normal profit will be considered as a cost and it is built into the average cost curve.

Costs can be looked at from the point of view of total costs, or the cost per unit, which is also known as average cost.

Now test yourself Tested

8 How much profit is normal profit?

9 How do you put normal profit on a diagram?

Answers on p. 109

Total costs

Revised

These can be split into two components: fixed costs which do not change with output, and variable costs which increase as more is produced. An example of a fixed cost is rent paid for a building. An example of a variable cost is raw materials, such as cocoa beans used to make chocolate. For the diagram and formulae of these and all the cost curves, see Table 1.2 on page 24. The gradient of the total cost curve is the marginal cost.

Typical mistake

It is very common to confuse total and average costs. Remember that total costs will never fall and unless they are fixed costs, they will always be rising (fixed costs stay constant as more is produced).

Average costs

Revised

Average cost is total cost divided by the amount produced, or quantity (Q). The cost per unit falls as more is produced because the fixed cost is spread out over more units of output. For example, if you are making chocolate bars, the more you produce the more the cost of the factory is spread out over the number of units produced.

Average fixed cost

Average fixed cost is the cost of overheads such as rent. These are spread out as more is produced. Because fixed costs do not change with output, then by definition fixed cost per unit must always fall.

Now test yourself Tested

10 Are wages fixed costs or variable costs?

Answers on p. 109

Examiner's tip

The gradient of the cost curve shows the increase in cost of producing one more unit. Because the cost curve is always rising (or zero), marginal cost is always positive (or zero) so you will never see marginal cost as a negative number.

Examiner's tip

It is useful to remember the initials of the average fixed cost (AFC) by noting that the words can be replaced with 'always falling curve' — initials AFC.

Average variable cost

Average variable costs are the costs per unit of the factors that change as more is produced. The shape of the average variable cost curve can be explained using the marginal cost curve which goes through the very lowest point of the average variable cost curve. When marginal cost is below average and variable costs, it means the cost of producing the next unit is less than the average cost of producing a unit. So this extra unit produced will bring down the average though by not as much.

Marginal cost

Revised

Here is an example to explain the relationship between the average and the marginal.

Imagine you are playing a game of cricket and the average batsman's score is 23. You go out to bat and you are having a bad day, caught for a golden duck and you are out. Your score is nil. It is also the marginal score and your score will pull down the average for your team. You will not pull them all down to your score, but you will shave a bit from the average of the team as a whole. Suppose you score 23? Your marginal score is the same as the average, so the average will remain the same. But if you have a fantastic innings, and you make 72, then your marginal score will pull up the batting average. It is exactly the same relationship with marginal cost and average variable cost. If the cost of producing one more is less than the average then the average cost will fall. If the marginal is the same as the average, then the average remains the same, and if the marginal is greater than the average then the average will rise.

Figure 1.2 illustrates this. Notice that when marginal cost is below average cost the marginal cost could be falling or rising, but average cost will still fall.

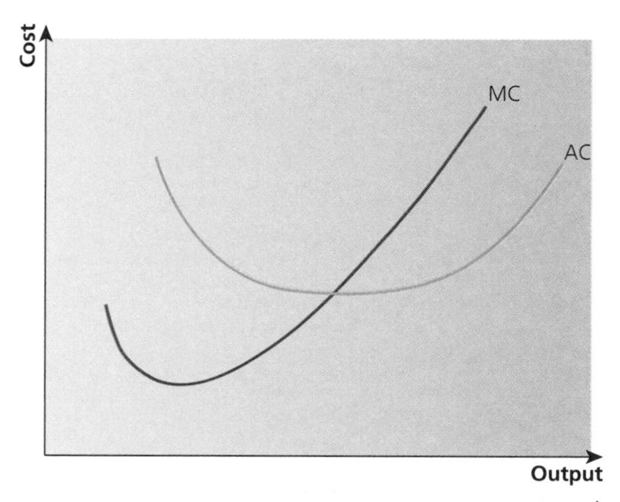

Figure 1.2 The relationship between MC and AC

What explains the shape of the marginal cost curve? The marginal cost curve looks a bit like a tick, or a Nike swoosh. While it might fall a little at the beginning, at some point it starts to rise, and from then it never stops rising. The increasing marginal cost is explained by the law of diminishing marginal returns.

Revision activity

Sketch some U-shaped average cost (AC) curves across a page. Then add marginal costs (MC). Check the MC looks like a Nike tick and goes through the lowest point on each AC.

Now test yourself Tested

11 Why do marginal cost curves eventually rise?

Answers on p. 109

Law of diminishing marginal returns

Revised

To be able to picture the **law of diminishing returns** in your mind, imagine a farmer with an orchard of 200 apple trees. Working alone, picking apples is a very time-consuming business. If you have someone with you, you can pass down the baskets of apples and someone can move the ladder for you. Some of the apples are hard to pick but some can be gathered easily without climbing the trees.

- The farmer measures his **marginal product** in terms of baskets of apples; these increase as he hires more labourers to pick the apples.

The **law of diminishing returns** says that as increasing units of a variable factor are added to a fixed factor, the marginal product eventually falls.

Marginal product is the extra output when one more factor of output is added.

- The **fixed factor** is the orchard; the **variable factor** is the workers. As more workers are taken on there might initially be a real benefit in having just a few pickers. So two workers might well produce more than double the quantity because of the teamwork and cooperation involved.
- In these very early stages of production, the marginal cost curve might even fall, that is the marginal product or the extra output increases when another worker is taken on.
- However, this scenario will reach a point where extra workers cannot increase the output as much as workers employed earlier in the stage of production. This is because the apples will be harder to pick because they are higher up the tree — all the easily picked apples have been collected — and remaining apples cost more time to pick.
- There is a fixed number of apples in the orchard which cannot be increased in the **short run**, so there must come a point at which it becomes more and more expensive to get the last apples.
- This is called the law of diminishing returns. It only operates in the short run because in the long run the farmer can plant more apple trees.

A **fixed factor** is the factor of production, such as the size of your apple orchard, which cannot be changed in the short run.

A **variable factor** is a resource, such as labourers picking crops, which costs more as the firm produces more.

The **short run** is the period of time in which at least one factor is fixed.

Now test yourself Tested

12 Can the marginal product ever fall?

Answers on p. 109

The relationship between the marginal cost curve and the average cost curve is explained in exactly the same way as the relationship between marginal cost and average variable cost. This is because the only difference between average variable cost and average cost is the average fixed cost which has absolutely no relationship with marginal cost.

Costs in the long run

Economies of scale

Revised

In the long run there are no fixed costs, that is, all costs are variable. Because there are no fixed costs, there cannot be the law of diminishing returns, which describes the relationship between inputs and outputs when factors are applied to a *fixed* cost. There are no laws to describe the pattern of costs in the long run, but there are some principles that are often observable, which we call the benefits of large-scale production, or economies of scale, where long-run average costs fall:

- **Managerial economies:** both large and small firms have just one person at the top, the risk-taker. While the manager of a bigger firm might earn more, there are bound to be some duplicated costs when two smaller firms combine to become a bigger one. Larger firms can afford better managers, ones with a good track record, and better management usually means higher profits or long-term sustainability.
- **Financial economies:** larger firms have access to a wider range of credit than small firms and usually at a lower price. Large firms can

issue shares on the stock market and can do deals with lenders to borrow at cheaper rates. Because they have more collateral, large firms are often seen as a safer bet for loans, in other words if their payments dry up there are more assets in the firm that can be sold to pay off the debt.

- **Commercial economies:** large firms can bulk-buy from their suppliers. Because they buy a large amount at a steady rate they are likely to get better deals. For example, Wal-Mart in the USA cuts a very cheap price from all its suppliers and that is how it keeps prices low.
- **Technical economies:** doubling the dimensions of any object increases the volume by eight times. So a larger warehouse, or a larger shop or lorry, can carry much more per square metre. You only need to look at the number of pantechnicons on the motorway to see the advantages of large-scale production.
- **Marketing economies:** as a firm grows bigger, the cost of advertising is spread out over a larger number of potential customers. For example, a national advert would not be suitable for a small firm, and a £20 million sponsorship deal with Newcastle United would not be possible for a firm like wonga.com if the market for pay-day loans were not as big as it is. (One million customers a year and rising, in the UK alone.)

Now test yourself Tested ☐

13 Get a pile of stock cubes or sugar lumps from the kitchen. Imagine these represent storage space in a warehouse. Take one and measure the volume, e.g. 1 cm^3. Now double the height, width and breadth of the warehouse. How many cubes do you use?

Answers on p. 109

Diseconomies of scale

Revised ☐

When firms become big they may in fact face rising long-run average costs.

- **Unwieldiness:** large firms can become difficult to manage, especially if they are operating in different countries with different cultures, time zones, languages and hours of working. When a firm is difficult to manage, we say it is unwieldy; decisions may take longer to implement and the person making the decision may not have knowledge of the outcome. Unions can become more powerful in a large organisation because they have greater ability to influence working patterns. It is very difficult to manage a large firm where some tasks become redundant, as people can be very keen to hold on to what they do.
- **Slowness:** it usually takes a large firm a long time to respond.
- **X-inefficiency** (see pages 19–20): lack of competition for a large firm may mean that costs are allowed to rise.
- **Communication:** one caricature of large firms involves lots of e-mails flying around and meetings-about-meetings. Often, this is all too true. Furthermore, workers may experience delays waiting for others to complete their tasks.
- **Lack of engagement:** in a large organisation the management may become very distant from the workers. Workers may then become less loyal to management and the purposes of the firm.

This may mean they take more days off sick, or spend working time inefficiently without seeing or feeling how this directly impacts on the firm's profit.

Now test yourself Tested

14 If diseconomies of scale have set in, what should the firm do?

Answers on p. 109

External economies of scale

Revised

Sometimes an industry as a whole grows, with the effect that individual firms can benefit from this growth. Firms based in the Tech City in East London are benefiting from super-fast broadband, new transport links and excellent publicity from the government which make it cheaper and more effective for any firm that is based there. The long-run average cost curve of the firm moves downwards without any action by the firm itself as the industry grows. Note, however, that as the industry grows, external diseconomies of scale may set in. For example, firms involved in direct marketing now find themselves in a market so flooded with players that it is very difficult for any one firm to be noticed.

Now test yourself Tested

15 What is the difference between internal and external economies of scale?

Answers on p. 109

Efficiency

Efficiency measures how well resources are used, that is, the output relative to some other factor, such as the cost of resources used.

Productive efficiency

Revised

Productive efficiency occurs where a firm operates on the lowest average cost, that is, the lowest point on the average cost curve. If the price is equal to average cost, then this is the lowest price that the customer can enjoy. So in terms of consumer surplus (welfare to the consumer), and effective use of factors of production, this is the optimum output. However, there is very little incentive for a firm to operate at productive efficiency and rarely any incentive to lower the price this far. It occurs where price is equal to marginal cost and equal to average cost. The reason MC = AC is because MC always crosses AC at its lowest point. See the marginal analysis on page 15.

Allocative efficiency

Revised

Allocative efficiency occurs where the price equals the marginal cost of production, that is P = MC. It means that people are paying the exact amount it costs to produce the last unit. The best way to consider this is the situation where it is not true: if people are prepared to pay more than it costs to produce the last unit then it would be better in terms of consumer satisfaction to produce more units — because consumers are prepared to pay more than the cost to society. By contrast, if the consumer satisfaction from the last unit is less than cost of making the unit, then production should be cut back, as consumers do not appreciate the costs involved.

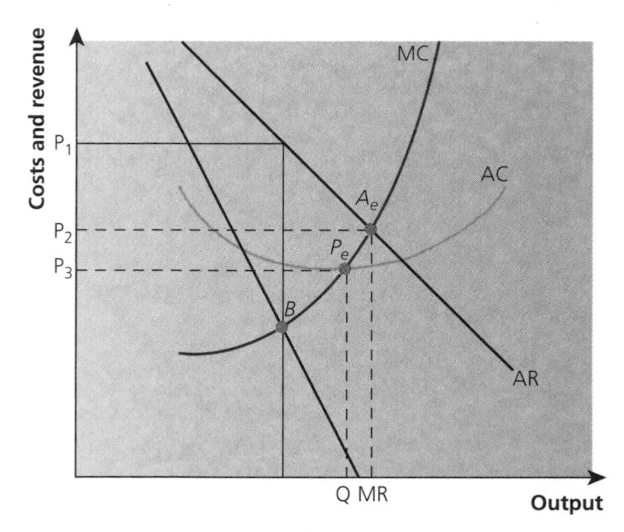

Figure 1.3 The relative prices and outputs of productive efficiency at P_3 and allocative efficiency at P_2. P_1 shows price for a profit-maximising firm, with B as the equilibrium point.

Now test yourself Tested

16 Could productive and allocative efficiency ever occur at the same point?

Answers on p. 109

Here is an example. You are making chocolates to sell in a market. Productive efficiency occurs when you get the costs down to a minimum — you spread out the fixed costs, and the rising labour costs do not yet outweigh the falling overheads. Allocative efficiency occurs if you stop making the product when making the last one is equal to the amount people will pay for the last chocolate on your stall at the end of the day. If it is a perfectly competitive market, these two points will be exactly the same in the long run. But usually productive efficiency kicks in at a lower output than allocative efficiency, as demand curves are downward sloping. Compare points for productive efficiency P_e and allocative efficiency A_e on Figure 1.3 above.

Typical mistake

Many students find it hard to point out productive efficiency on a graph because they do not draw the MC going through the lowest point of AC. If you have drawn it correctly, MC = AC at productive efficiency, the lowest point on AC.

X-inefficiency

Revised

This is when costs rise because there is no competition. If you are taking a course at school for which there is no exam you tend to try less hard and never do any homework. This is because there is no competition. When you compete with other students in an exam, you work harder. So it is with firms — especially those subsidised or owned by the public sector; when costs start rising there is little incentive to cut back. If wages and employment are not dependent on revenues the workers might not work as hard to raise the volume of sales. See pages 37–39 on ways in which the public sector might try to reduce x-inefficiency by trying to increase competition in markets.

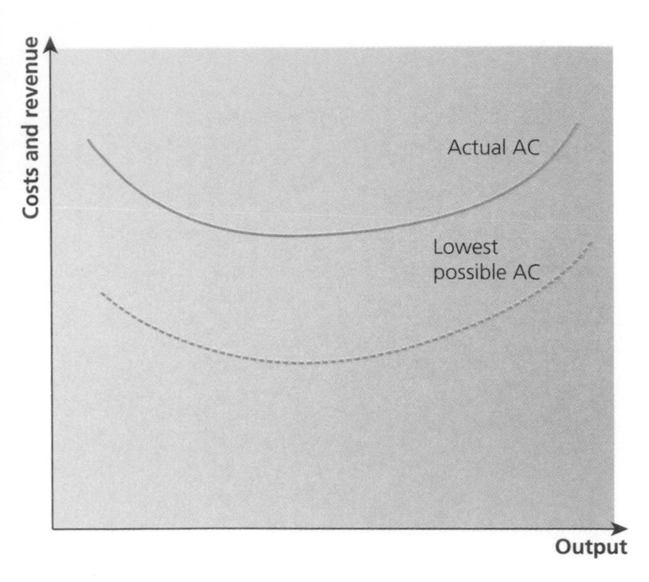

Figure 1.4 X-inefficiency on actual AC.

Profit

What is meant by profit?

Revised

Profit is the reward for risk-taking. There are two types of profit:

- **Normal profit:** this is the minimum necessary to keep the risk-taking resources in their current use. It is built into the average cost curve, and represents the cost of use of the entrepreneurship factor of production. Normal profit occurs when AC = AR or TC = TR. It does not act as a signal for other firms to enter the market, nor does it cause firms to want to leave the market. The size of normal profit varies according to the level of risk involved, and the other investment opportunities available at the time. If you are running your own business 'up-cycling' furniture then you probably do not need much profit to keep you in work — just enough to prevent you having to find a job working for someone else. But if you are running an oil exploration firm with a 20-year investment cycle then your normal profits will be much higher for you to keep your money in the business. In the first example, normal profit might be £8 000 a year and in the second £8 000 million.
- **Supernormal profit:** this is profit above the minimum required to stay in business. It is the difference between TR and TC.

Profit maximisation

Revised

Profit maximisation occurs where the firm cannot increase its profits, either by increasing or decreasing price or output. It is best explained using marginal analysis. For this, you must first understand the key terms marginal cost, marginal revenue and **marginal profit** (see the definitions given in the key term box on page 8).

Marginal profit is the extra profit gained from selling one more unit, or MP = MR – MC.

This is the profit maximisation point: MR = MC. You can rearrange this formula to MR – MC = 0. See the definition of marginal profit in the key term box. You may also observe that MR = MC when the gradients of the total cost curve and the total revenue curves are the same. Because these are concave to each other this must also be the point at which they are furthest apart. This can be explained using Figure 1.5.

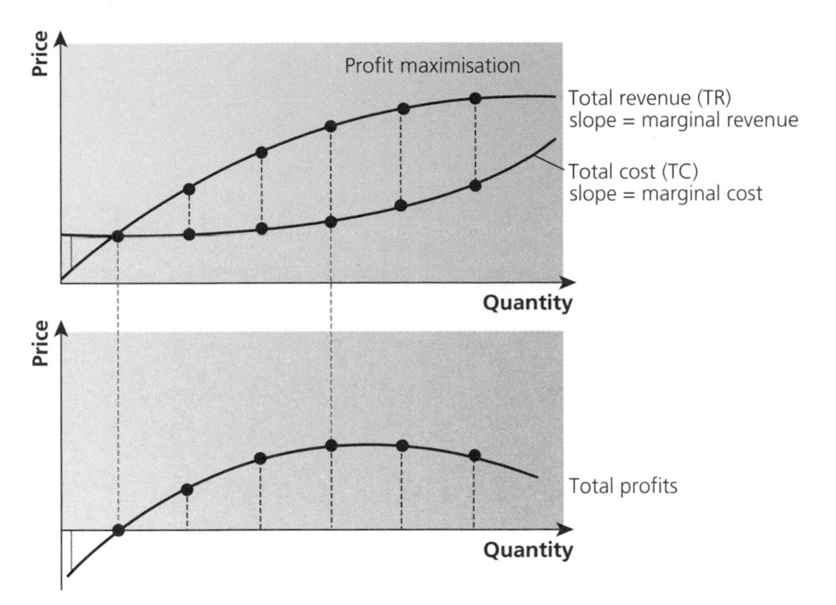

Figure 1.5 The greatest distance apart for TR and TC is where profit maximisation occurs. Notice the gradients of TR and TC are the same, that is, MR = MC

Profit maximisation occurs where the cost of making one more unit is exactly equal to the revenue gained from selling that unit.

Consider the situation if a firm produced at a different output than this:

- At a lower output, marginal revenue is greater than the cost of producing that unit. There is more profit to be made. That is, the marginal profit is greater than zero. A rational firm would not stop producing when MR > MC because there is more money just waiting to be made.
- Likewise consider the situation if a firm is producing at an output higher than MR = MC. The cost of making another unit is more than the revenue received from selling it. The marginal profit is negative. The firm should cut back production, and it is actually giving away its profits if MC > MR.

It follows that logically the firm should operate at MR = MC, and the reasoning in this paragraph is called marginal analysis.

Examiner's tip

Use marginal analysis in your exam. Examiners like it — it is an efficient way of showing that you understand and you are not just reciting a textbook.

Now test yourself Tested

17 What happens when marginal profit is zero?

Answers on p. 109

Barriers to entry and exit

- **Barriers to entry** are any obstacles that prevent a firm setting up, or extending its reach into new markets.
- **Barriers to exit** are any factors which prevent firms leaving a market, or make it more unprofitable to leave than stay in business, even if they are operating at a loss. Examples include sunk costs, which are irretrievable costs such as advertising or the value of the goodwill in a business.

Types of barriers

Revised

There are three main types:

1. Some are deliberately imposed and can be seen by the regulators as illegal anti-competitive measures:
   - predatory pricing
   - limit pricing
2. Many barriers to entry exist simply due to the nature of the business or the market, for example:
   - economies of scale, minimum efficient scale
3. Some barriers to entry are actually imposed by the authorities, in cases where too much competition might be seen as working against the interest of the consumer:
   - legal barriers, such as patents
   - state-owned franchises, such as the train operating companies
   - legislation to allow firms to operate, such as 4G licences

As an example of a barrier to exit, let's take a butcher who is making a loss. He can sell the shop but this might be difficult in a recession as people might not be able to find the credit, or be unwilling to take the risk. He can sell his specialised equipment, but the second-hand market is also unreliable in a recession for reaching the values that might normally be expected. But probably worst of all, the reputation that the butcher has built up over the years, with loyal customers, good service records and word-of-mouth recommendations, are goodwill elements that cannot be sold on with the firm.

If barriers to entry and exit are high, the firms are likely to be operating with strong market power. The market is likely to be a monopoly if the barriers to entry are extremely high (for example Apple computers face no direct competition and have some product lines which are strongly dominating the market). If the barriers to entry are high but not impossible to overcome then the firms are likely to be operating in an oligopoly (see page 32). If barriers to entry are low then the firm is operating in a fairly contestable market, and might be in monopolistic competition or, in the case of no barriers to entry and exit, the market is perfectly contestable, as in perfect competition.

Now test yourself

Tested

18 Are barriers to entry the only factor determining market power?

Answers on p. 109

Measuring market concentration

Concentration ratios

Revised

Market power is most effectively measured using a concentration ratio. The **n-firm concentration ratio** measures the proportion of the market dominated by the *largest n firms*. For example, the US retail banking market is highly fragmented and has a very low concentration ratio. This is illustrated by the fact that the top 12 US banks held only about 35% of the market share based on total US deposits. This means the 12-firm concentration ratio is 35%, very unlike the UK market where five firms have control of around 70% of the retail banking sector.

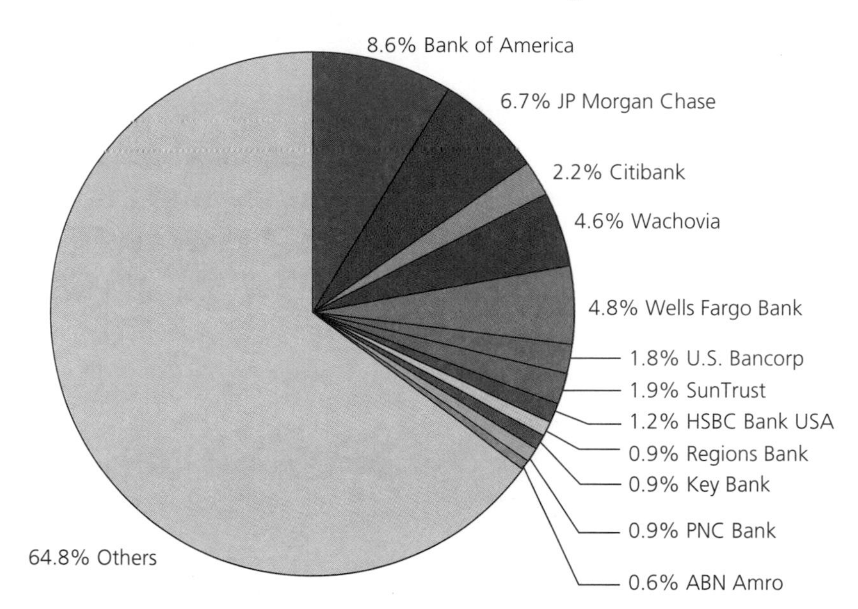

Figure 1.6 The market share of retail banks in the US

Examiner's tip

Exam questions often mislead students by providing a list of major players in a market and bunching together the smallest, less significant firms under the title 'other'. Many students count 'other' in their calculation, as the total of 'other' might well occupy a bigger section than some of the biggest firms. Be careful not to include 'other'.

Exam practice

Data-response question

Extract: Starbucks

Starbucks, the Seattle-based group, with a market capitalization of $40 billion, is the second-largest restaurant or cafe chain globally after McDonald's. Accounts filed by its UK subsidiary show that since it opened in the UK in 1998 the company has racked up over £3 billion ($4.8 billion) in coffee sales, and opened 735 outlets but paid only £8.6 million in income taxes, and these only because the taxman disallowed some deductions.

Over the past three years, Starbucks has reported no profit, and paid no income tax, on sales of £1.2 billion in the UK. McDonald's, by comparison, had a tax bill of over £80 million on £3.6 billion of UK sales. Kentucky Fried Chicken, part of Yum Brands Inc., the no. 3 global restaurant or cafe chain by market capitalization, incurred taxes of £36 million on £1.1 billion in UK sales, according to the accounts of their UK units.*

Yet transcripts of investor and analyst calls over 12 years show Starbucks officials regularly talked about the UK business as 'profitable', said they were very pleased with it, or even cited it as an example to follow for operations back home in the United States.

Source: extract from *Special Report: How Starbucks avoids UK taxes* by Tom Bergin, 15 October 2012, Reuters

**The corporation tax rate in the UK is currently 25% but the Starbucks bill is totally legal, because the tax is a percentage of profit not revenue. The difference is fixed costs, and Starbucks has been able to declare overhead costs to wipe out the 'profits' through a number of payments which Starbucks must make to subsidiaries abroad. This includes a 4.7% premium to the Dutch division of Starbucks — the regional headquarters — for rights images and the coffee recipes. It buys the coffee beans from the company's Swiss operation at a 20% premium, paying tax in Switzerland at just 12%. The company says it pays higher prices because it spends £315 million annually on tax-deductible areas such as research and development. It says the cost of rent on its UK stores is very high, and the firm spends more on store layout and design than rival firms.*

1 Using examples from the passage, examine the functions of profit in terms of business efficiency. **[8]**

2 Using an appropriate cost and revenue diagram, discuss **one** reason why a firm such as Starbucks can be shown to have a profit and a loss at the same time. **[16]**

Answers and quick quizzes online

Online

Examiner's summary

Table 1.1 summarises the definitions, formulae and explanations that you need to know for the theory of individual firms. Revenues and costs are covered in Table 1.2

Table 1.1 Theory of individual firms

Term	Formula	Explanation
Total profit	TR – TC or (AR – AC) × Q	Supernormal, abnormal or subnormal (a loss).
Normal profit	TR = TC or AR = AC	Return to the entrepreneur is built into the cost curve, which is just enough profit to keep the entrepreneur in this function.
Profit maximisation	MR = MC	Marginal profit is zero; or the vertical difference between TR and TC is at a maximum.
Sales maximisation	AC = AR or TR = TC when costs cross revenue from below	Highest level of output consistent with normal profit.
Revenue maximisation	MR = 0	Maximum total revenue. Selling another unit adds the same to total revenue as the amount lost from units being sold at a lower price.
Price taker/perfectly elastic demand	AR = MR	TR straight line going through zero, AR and MR horizontal. Price elasticity of demand is infinite.
Price maker/ monopoly	AR > MR	AR downward sloping, MR twice gradient. The firm has some degree of price-setting power.
Break even	AR = AC	Firm covers costs, and makes only normal profit.
Shut down	AR = AVC	Firm covers AVC only, makes a loss. If price is above this but below AC there is a loss but the firm *contributes* to AFC so carries on in the short run.
Productive efficiency	MC = AC	Minimum point on AC, lowest cost per unit.
Allocative efficiency	P = MC	Price charged maximises social welfare, taking into account consumer and producer surplus.

Table 1.2 Revenues and costs

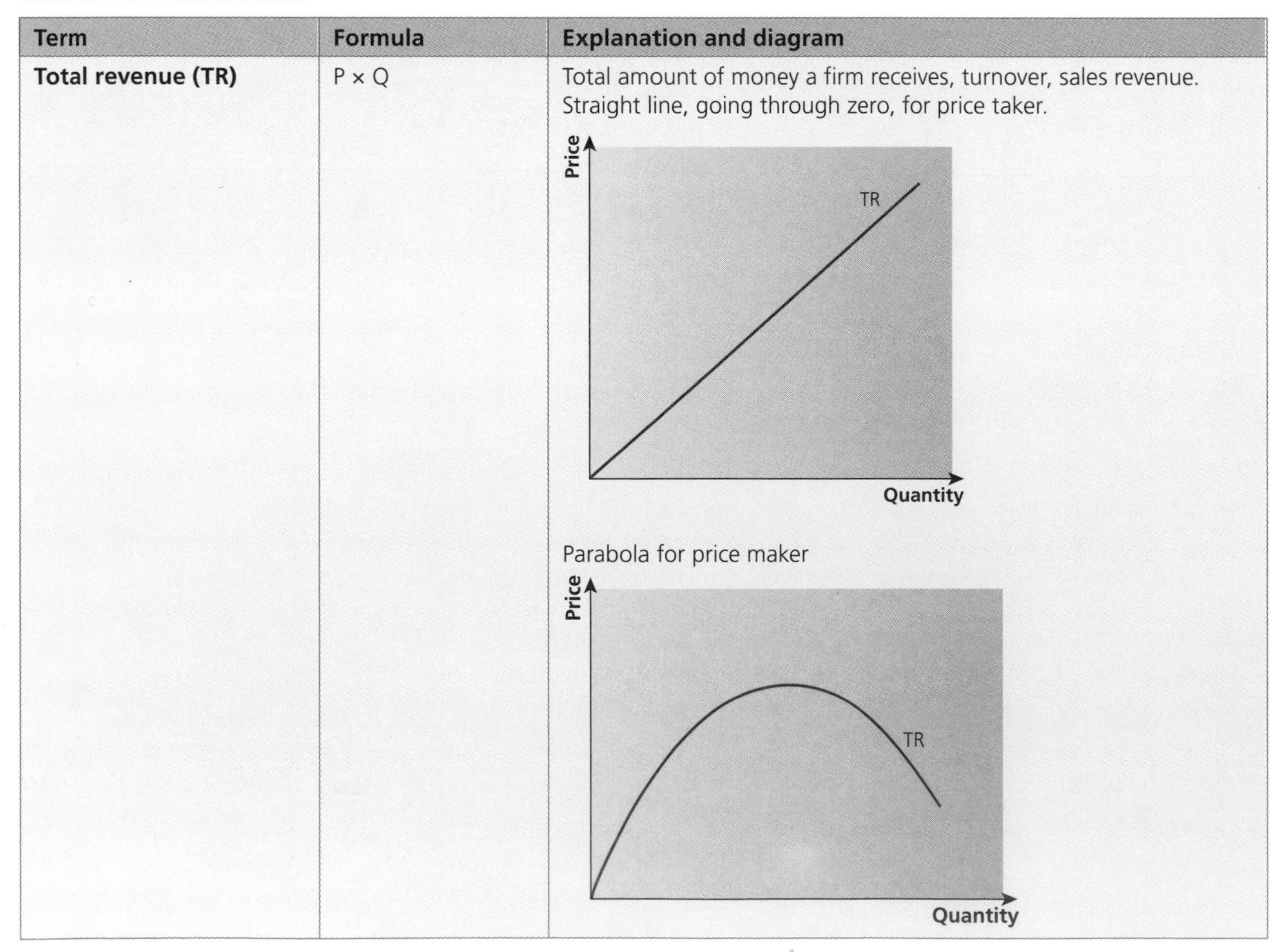

Term	Formula	Explanation and diagram
Total revenue (TR)	P × Q	Total amount of money a firm receives, turnover, sales revenue. Straight line, going through zero, for price taker. Parabola for price maker

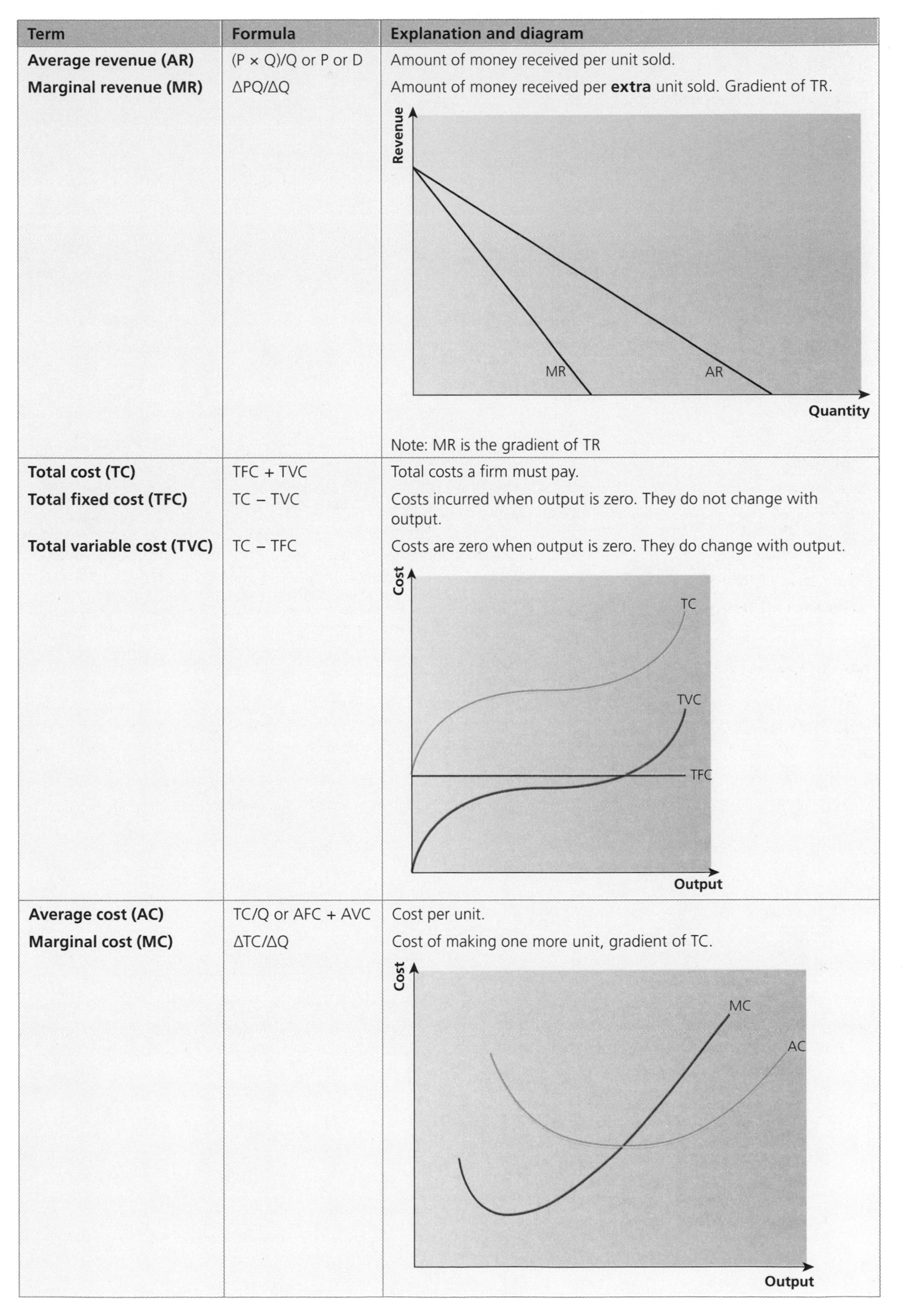

Term	Formula	Explanation and diagram
Average revenue (AR)	(P × Q)/Q or P or D	Amount of money received per unit sold.
Marginal revenue (MR)	ΔPQ/ΔQ	Amount of money received per **extra** unit sold. Gradient of TR. Note: MR is the gradient of TR
Total cost (TC)	TFC + TVC	Total costs a firm must pay.
Total fixed cost (TFC)	TC – TVC	Costs incurred when output is zero. They do not change with output.
Total variable cost (TVC)	TC – TFC	Costs are zero when output is zero. They do change with output.
Average cost (AC)	TC/Q or AFC + AVC	Cost per unit.
Marginal cost (MC)	ΔTC/ΔQ	Cost of making one more unit, gradient of TC.

Continued

Continued

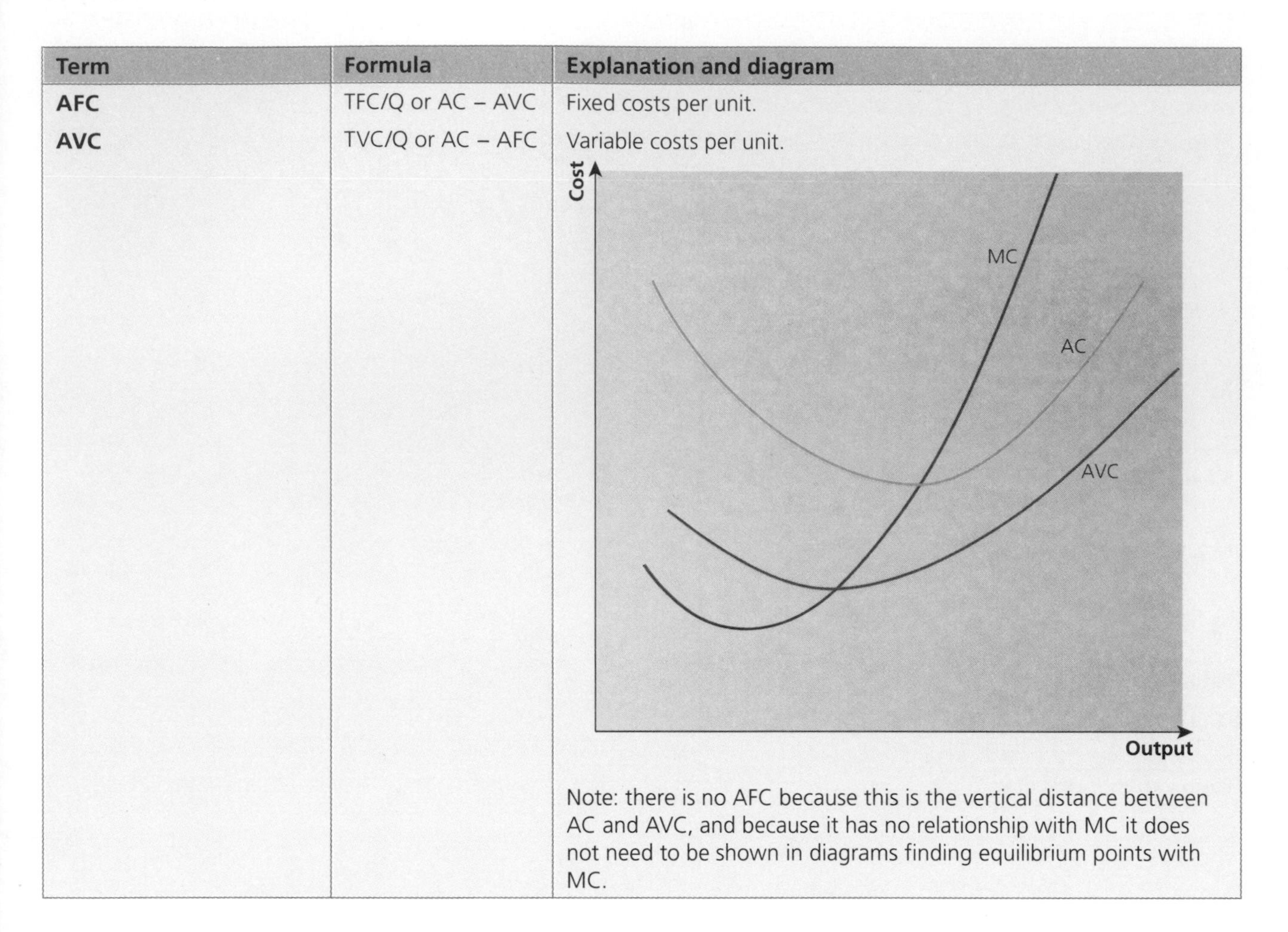

Term	Formula	Explanation and diagram
AFC	TFC/Q or AC – AVC	Fixed costs per unit.
AVC	TVC/Q or AC – AFC	Variable costs per unit. Note: there is no AFC because this is the vertical distance between AC and AVC, and because it has no relationship with MC it does not need to be shown in diagrams finding equilibrium points with MC.

2 The firm in the market

In this chapter we look at the market structure that firms operate in. If a firm sells products similar to those of other firms, it operates in a competitive market. But if it has a unique product or has strong barriers to entry it operates with some market power, also known as monopoly power.

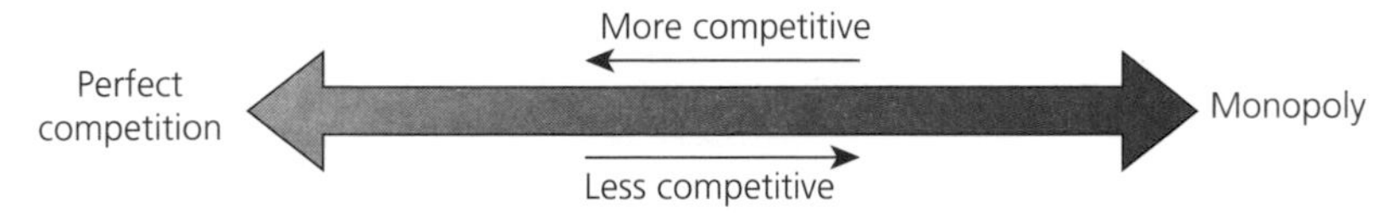

Figure 2.1 Spectrum of competition

Perfect competition

The model of perfect competition

Revised

The model of perfect competition is a model of an extreme form of competition. In this model, certain assumptions hold:

- There are many buyers and sellers. Neither buyers nor sellers can influence the price. We say they are price takers, and firms face a horizontal demand curve AR = MR.
- There are no barriers to entry or exit.
- There is perfect knowledge or information, e.g. about production techniques and sources of cheap raw materials.
- All firms aim to maximise profits, MR = MC.

To draw a diagram for perfect competition, we draw the individual firm facing a horizontal demand curve AR = MR. This means it has no market power, no influence over price. It is also very helpful to add a diagram showing the whole market, that is, the industry demand and supply. Here price is determined, and the demand as a whole is determined by consumer preferences, showing that as price falls, people demand more.

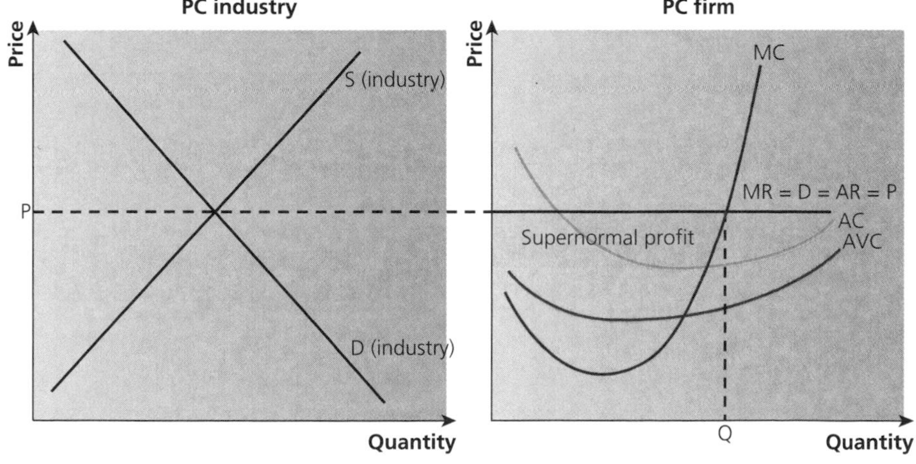

Figure 2.2 Perfectly competitive industry and firm, with short-run supernormal profits being made. Other firms will enter the industry

In Figure 2.2 the firm is enjoying a price which is above the average costs of production. The firm is making supernormal profit. This is shown by the area shaded in blue. However the profit acts as a signal to other firms to enter the industry. There are no barriers to entry, so nothing will stop other firms entering. So this excessive profit will soon disappear and we will end up in long-run equilibrium.

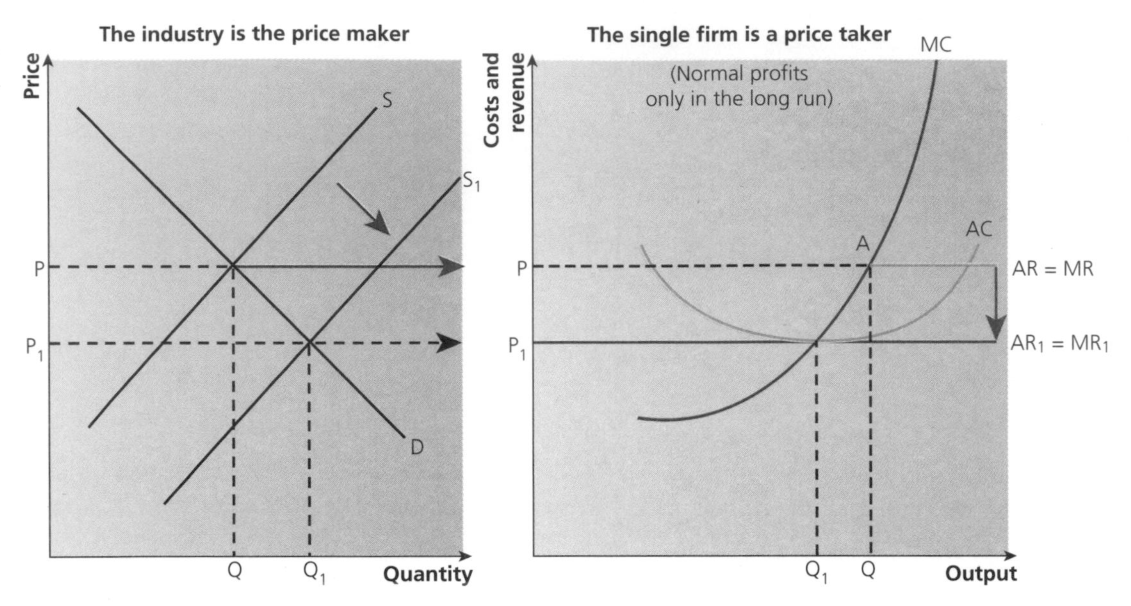

Figure 2.3 Long-run equilibrium

Note that for the individual firm, prices fall, and also output falls from Q to Q_1. This is because at lower prices it will want to operate at a slightly slower output (MC is lower because MR is lower) but overall the industry supply has increased from Q to Q_1 because there are more firms in the industry.

Firms making a loss

Revised

Now look at the situation where the perfectly competitive firm is making a loss. Here firms will start leaving the industry, prices will rise, but for the individual firm the output will actually rise. This is because there are fewer firms in the market and each one makes just a little more, allowing MC to rise as MR rises. Remember that MC always equals MR.

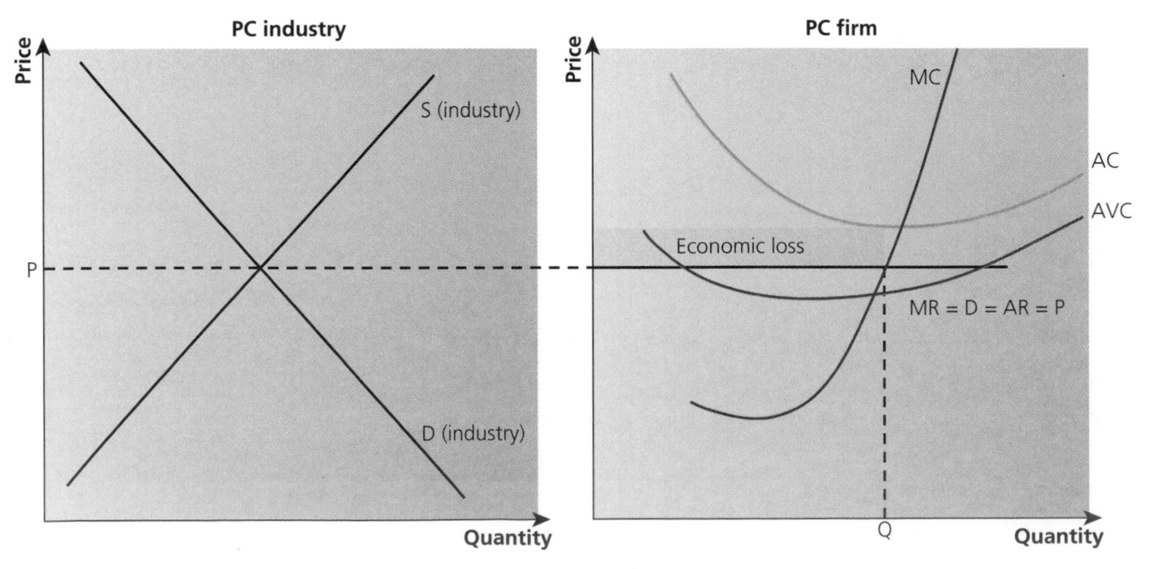

Figure 2.4 Perfectly competitive industry and firm, with short-run losses being made. Firms will leave the industry until the losses disappear

Does the firm in perfect competition automatically shut down when it makes a loss? We know there are no barriers to exit so it seems sensible for the firm to leave the industry straight away. However before this long-run scenario plays out, there is the short run to consider. A perfectly competitive firm will have fixed costs in the short run. These will have to be paid even if the firm shuts down immediately. The question for the firm is whether a larger loss will be made by shutting down completely (paying the fixed costs) or waiting until the fixed costs become variable.

To discover what the firm should do we look at the shut-down point. This occurs when the price the firm receives covers its average variable costs (AVC). If the firm more than covers its AVC then we say it is making a **contribution** to the fixed costs of production. But if it cannot even cover its AVC, it is better to shut down straightaway; it would make less of a loss if it does not produce at all.

Here is an example. You are running a theatre company that is looking for venues to run the show. The venues have to be paid whether the show runs or not and is a fixed cost. The actors are variable costs — if you don't put on the show (and you give them enough notice) you will not have to pay for them. You try selling tickets and realise you are not going to make a profit. Should the show go on? If you have sold enough tickets to pay for the actors then you should run the show, as you will pay a contribution towards the fixed cost of hiring the venue. But if you have not even sold enough tickets to pay for the players, it is better for you if they stay at home.

Now test yourself

1 Why do firms carry on producing even if they are making a loss?

Answers on p. 109

Tested

Monopoly

A **pure monopoly** exists where there is only one firm supplying a good or service. It is often more practical to use the **legal** definition of monopoly, that a firm supplies at least 25% of the market.

Pure monopoly involves one firm alone dominating the market.

In a **legal monopoly**, one firm dominates 25% or more of the market.

Assumptions of pure monopoly:

- one firm in the market
- high barriers to entry and exit
- firms aim for profit maximisation MR = MC
- firms face a downward-sloping demand curve

Benefits and costs of monopoly

Revised

There may be advantages to many **stakeholders** when a monopoly exists.

A **stakeholder** is any person or group that has a vested interest in a firm. It includes consumers, suppliers, owners e.g. shareholders, the government (receivers of corporation tax) and other firms already supplying in the market.

Benefits of monopolies

For consumers:

- Innovation — bringing in new ideas and processes, and being able to take the risks of new ideas not working.
- Research and development — large firms plough back enormous sums into this high-risk enterprise; research more often than not leads to failure so only large firms with monopoly profits can afford to take the risk.
- Investment — large-scale firms can and will afford to invest, often because they have confidence that they will still be in existence to reap the rewards.

For governments:

- Large firms pay higher rates of **corporation tax**. The more profit the monopoly makes the more the firm will pay in tax.
- Monopolies might have many competitors outside the country. Monopoly power helps to keep jobs within the country and may improve the balance of payments.

Corporation tax is tax on profits.

For workers:

- Monopolies might offer better job security.
- Higher profits for the firm might mean higher bonuses or perks for the workers.

For other firms such as suppliers:

- A monopoly can offer a secure outlet for suppliers. If your company makes car tyres then a monopoly car producer could keep the orders rolling in.
- Firms which buy from monopolies might be more likely to have consistent quality. It is not worth a monopoly taking any risks with the quality of a well-known brand, as there is too much to lose.

Costs of monopolies

For consumers:

- Less choice — large firms keep to the brands that make the most profit. Unprofitable brands soon come off the shelves.
- Higher prices — monopolists can increase price to maximise their profits.
- Lower quality — firms with no competition might not have the incentive to produce better goods or services, and the after-care service might be limited. The good thing about competition in the case of a bank, for instance, is that if you do not get the service you need you can change bank.

Examiner's tip

You can use the arguments against monopolies as evaluation points in an argument assessing the case *for* monopolies.

For governments:

- Monopolies can find it easy to avoid paying tax, and can employ expensive tax consultants to help them do so.

For workers:

- In a monopoly the worker does not have strong bargaining power. If he or she is not happy, it might not be easy to transfer to a similar company, as there is just one employer in that industry. Wages might also be kept down for this reason.
- Monopoly workers do not necessarily have any more job security than in more competitive industries. Monopoly profits can be used to invest in new machinery which can replace workers.

For other firms:

- Firms which buy from monopolies can be exploited. Small computer outlets, for instance, have no choice over range and price when dealing with Apple products.
- Other firms can be deliberately forced out of the market (by limit pricing or predatory pricing) because they have not yet had the chance to establish themselves.

Now test yourself

2 Why do governments want to limit the power of monopolies?

Answers on p. 109

Tested

Price discrimination by a monopoly firm

Revised

Price discrimination occurs when a firm with some degree of market power charges more than one price for the same good or service.

In the model for price discrimination there are three conditions:

- There are different submarkets with different price elasticities of demand.
- Consumers cannot move between the submarkets — we say there is no 'arbitrage'.
- The cost of keeping the markets separate is less than the increased profits gained from so doing.

In the diagram we draw two separate submarkets, one with relatively inelastic demand and one with price elastic demand. We can plot the demand marginal revenue in the industry as a whole by combining the demand and marginal revenues from the two submarkets. The equilibrium for the two submarkets can be found from the industry market where MC equals MR in the third diagram (see Figure 2.5). This is the marginal cost the firm will operate at, but not the marginal revenue. For this we need to draw out the marginal revenue, that is, pull a line out to the left from the diagram on the right.

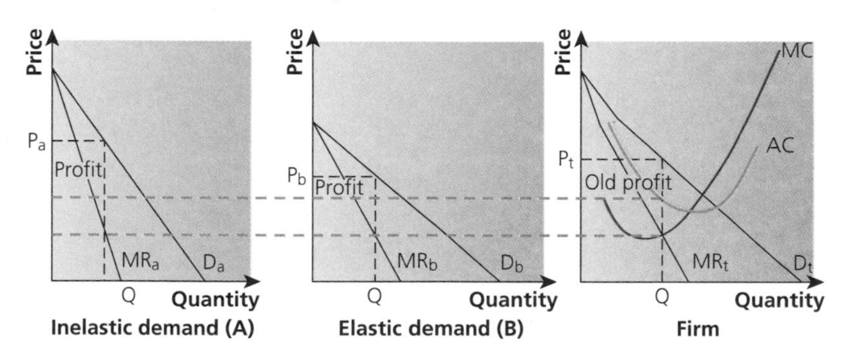

Figure 2.5 Price discrimination in two separate submarkets, A and B, with the firm as a whole shown in the third set of axes

When the marginal cost hits the marginal revenue in each of the other two markets (MR_a and MR_b), we draw a vertical line to show the quantity (Q) in each of the submarkets. The vertical line is extended upwards and meets the demand in each of the two markets, and we find the price in each market P_a and P_b. The price is higher in the relatively inelastic demand market.

Examiner's tip

Do not confuse price discrimination with the more common product discrimination, where different prices are charged for slightly different products. For example meals for children are half price at Ikea — but the meals are much smaller than the adult meals.

Examiner's tip

Always make sure the price is higher in the relatively price inelastic market, and lower in the more price elastic market.

Now test yourself

3 Why is price discrimination focused on markets with monopoly power?

Answers on p. 109

Tested

Monopsony

A **pure monopsony** is a firm which is the sole buyer of resources or supplies. Many firms have *some* degree of monopsony power, which means firms have *some control* over their suppliers.

Examiner's tip

You do not need to be able to draw or interpret a monopsony diagram in your exam, although you might find one more efficient than just using words. Any valid economics you use can earn credit, even if it is not required in your course.

Benefits of monopsony

Revised

The benefits of monopsony to firms and consumers include:

- Power in buying means the firm can make more profits as suppliers cannot overcharge.

- Lower buying costs might be passed on to the consumer in retail prices.
- Higher profits of monopsony can be used to invest and innovate.
- Monopsony power can give power to buyers in the face of monopoly supply of resources. For example, cosmetic producers such as L'Oréal can charge very high prices for their products but monopsonistic supermarkets can force them to cut their costs.

Costs of monopsony

Revised

The costs of monopsony to firms and consumers include:

- Suppliers can be squeezed out of business.
- Choice for consumers could be limited, as monopsony acts as a barrier to entry for new firms.
- Higher profits of monopsony can mean inequality.
- Firms might be investigated by the competition authorities.

Examiner's tip

You need to know the possible benefits and costs of monopsony power, in the context of data provided.

Now test yourself

Tested

4 What is the difference between monopoly power and monopsony power?

Answers on p. 109

Oligopoly

Oligopoly is a word of Greek origin: *oligo* means 'a few' and *poly* means 'sellers', so it means a few firms are dominating the market.

Assumptions

Revised

The assumptions of oligopoly are similar to monopoly, but with one key difference:

- A few firms dominate the market (the concentration ratios are *high*).
- There are high barriers to entry and exit.
- Firms aim for profit maximisation — MR = MC.
- The firm faces a downward-sloping demand curve.
- The firms are **interdependent**. This means that the actions of one firm are dependent on the actions of another. A firm's decisions on price, output and other competitive activities, such as the level of advertising, can have an immediate effect on competitors.

Examiner's tip

There is an 'f-rule' to help you decide whether a firm is operating in an oligopolistic market: 'Five or Fewer Firms control Fifty per cent of the market'. That is, if the concentration ratio (see page 22) is above 50% then there is likely to be an oligopoly.

Interdependence means that the actions of one agent depend upon the actions of another.

Now test yourself

Tested

5 Two firms each have 26% of a market. Is this monopoly, oligopoly, or something else?

Answers on p. 109

Game theory

Revised

This last assumption means that we can use **game theory** to analyse and evaluate the actions of firms in oligopoly. Game theory is a set of ideas which looks at strategies firms use to make decisions, for example on prices or levels of advertising.

Game theory is the study of strategies used to make decisions.

A **pay-off matrix** is a simple two-firm, two-outcome model.

Simple pay-off matrix

Two petrol stations, R and Q, are situated on the high street leading out of town. The price one charges is highly dependent upon the price charged by the other, and vice versa, as shown in the **pay-off matrix** in Figure 2.6.

		Q: High price	Q: Low price
R	High price	R £100 / Q £100	R 0 / Q £160
R	Low price	R £160 / Q 0	R £80 / Q £80

Figure 2.6 Simple pay-off matrix

If R and Q agree to charge a high price, they can make supernormal profits per hour of £100. R sees more money can be made and decides to undercut Q. R then gets £160 and Q gets nothing. Q is very unhappy so Q cuts prices too. Both firms find they get only £80 each. Not a very satisfactory conclusion! Perhaps they should both collude again and get £100 each.

As you can see there is a dilemma here. It seems to be worth **colluding**, and also worth breaking the collusion. Once the collusion is broken, it is worth colluding again. This is the **prisoner's dilemma** in action, and explains why **cartels** might form and why they might also be broken.

Non-collusive behaviour occurs when firms act in a way that does not involve collaboration with other players in the market. The kinked demand curve theory explained below provides an example.

A **prisoner's dilemma** is a model used in game theory to question whether firms might not collude, even if it appears that it is in their best interests to do so, or vice versa.

Cartels involve firms acting as one through an agreement.

Pricing strategies used in oligopoly

Revised

- **Price wars:** these occur when price cutting leads to retaliation and other firms cut prices, meaning the original firms again want to cut prices to increase their sales. As the name suggests, these can be destructive for all firms involved.
- **Predatory pricing:** this involves cutting prices below the average cost of production (this can also mean prices are below average variable costs). It is a short-term measure only, and once other firms have been forced out of the market the firm raises prices back up again. This is almost always illegal.
- **Limit pricing:** this involves cutting the price to the point where new possible entrants or newly entered higher-cost firms cannot compete. The incumbent firm (the one already in business and engaging in limit pricing) can sustain this position in the long term because it has lower costs. This may or may not be illegal, depending on the specific cases looked at by the competition authorities.
- **Price leadership:** in some markets the dominant firm acts to change prices and others will follow. This is because if other firms try to make changes, this could set off a price war or other sorts of retaliation. The

large firm becomes the established leader. Barclays bank has often been regarded as a price leader when it comes to setting inter-bank borrowing rates.

- **Non-price competition:** this takes place when firms take action to compete without changing the price of their products. This might be through advertising, loyalty cards, free gifts or similar strategies.

Examiner's tip

When students talk about non-collusive behaviour they tend to avoid using important economic theory such as brand loyalty reducing price elasticity of demand. The more economic theory you use in your answer, the more marks you can earn.

Collusion

Revised

This occurs when firms operate together, or collaborate. There are two types you need to know about for your exam:

- **Overt collusion:** overt means open; collusion means operating together. Overt collusion occurs if a firm sends messages to another firm about its prices or other decisions. It is illegal, and easier to detect than tacit collusion.
- **Tacit collusion:** tacit means quiet, or unspoken; collusion means operating together. An implicit understanding might operate between firms. For example when bidding at an auction there might be a gentleman's agreement — you won't bid as you won the last item, so allowing someone else to get a slightly lower price. This is also illegal, but very hard for the competition authorities to control.

Now test yourself

6 A finance director in a firm e-mails her counterpart in a competing firm and asks her what price rises are being planned for the Christmas period. What sort of collusion is this?

Answers on p. 109

Tested

Kinked demand theory

Revised

This is a neat model which can also be used to explain the behaviour of oligopolistic firms.

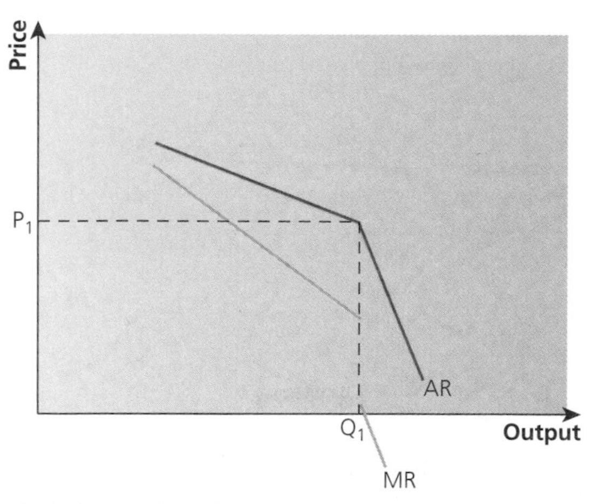

Figure 2.7 Kinked demand theory

The kinked demand curve explains why some prices are 'sticky' — that is, several firms might be charging the same price, and even if costs change the prices do not tend to change. Assume we start at point P_1 and Q_1 in Figure 2.7 above. Will firms increase revenue by either raising or lowering prices? According to this theory, no. Raising prices would not be copied by other firms and demand is relatively elastic. Cutting prices would be copied. An example is the price of bread and milk in supermarkets, which is often the same in Tesco, Sainsbury's and Morrisons. If the supermarkets raised the prices of these essential items, word would get around that these are the supermarkets that charge more, and demand would drop significantly (high level of price elasticity of demand) if prices were raised.

Examiner's tip

A note about the drawing of MR in Figure 2.7. If MR is drawn fully below zero it means that the price elasticity of demand is less than 1, that is, the firm makes less revenue by cutting its price. This means it is definitely not worth the firm cutting prices. However you can also draw MR above zero. While the price elasticity of demand is not technically inelastic, it is still not worth the firm cutting price because MC will be far below MR. So either way of drawing MR is acceptable, above or below zero, as long as you are careful in the way you describe what happens to total revenue.

However if prices were cut in one supermarket, the other firms are likely to follow suit immediately. That is, there is a different action or response when prices are raised or if they are cut, and neither action increases total revenue for the firm. The model explains why firms might look as if there is collusion but in fact nothing illegal is happening.

Evaluation of the model

The model does not explain why the prices are what they are in the first place. It only explains some degree of stability, and some markets are far more complex. A pay-off matrix gives a far wider range of possibilities and explains cartels and collusion. But the model can provide some simple game theory analysis when required.

Examiner's tip

The kinked demand theory is not required for your exam, but many students find it a logical and easily evaluated concept which can be used to pick up the marks in a question on oligopoly.

Now test yourself Tested

7 A firm is operating on the kink of a kinked demand curve. What can a firm do to price to raise its revenue? What would you advise this firm to do to increase its profits?

Answers on p. 109

Contestability

The threat of competition

Revised

Contestability is a measure of the ease with which firms can enter or exit an industry.

- High barriers to entry and exit make a market less contestable.
- Sunk costs are the key reason for low contestability. Any costs which cannot be recouped such as goodwill (see page 21) reduce contestability.
- A high level of competitiveness may be a sign that barriers to entry are low, but this is not the same concept. Even a monopoly can be perfectly contestable, if it is the only firm in an industry that no other firm wishes to enter because profits are low.
- A high level of concentration is a sign that contestability is low.

Signs of a high level of contestability include:

- low levels of supernormal profits
- low barriers to entry or exit
- low concentration ratios
- low sunk costs
- low levels of collusion or other signs of oligopoly
- new firms entering or leaving the market

Typical mistake

Many students confuse competitiveness and contestability, or concentration and contestability.

Examiner's tip

Make sure you can evaluate whether a market is contestable or not. If you are provided with some data you will be able to give evidence on both sides of the argument.

Now test yourself Tested

8 What are the benefits of high levels of contestability?

Answers on p. 109

Exam practice

Data-response question

Extract: Entry costs to London Dungeons, 2012

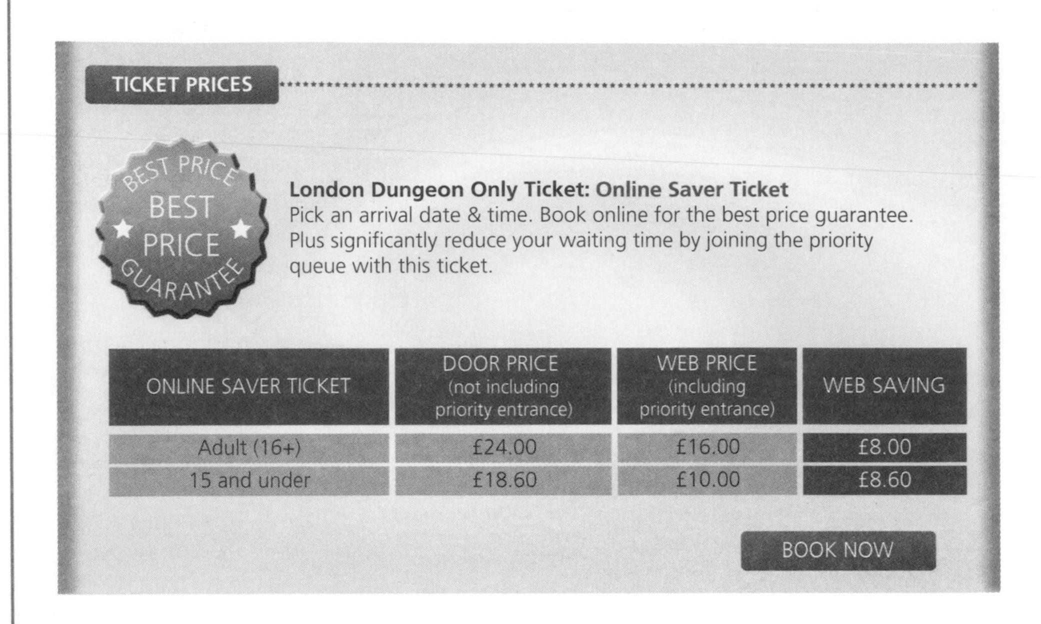
TICKET PRICES

BEST PRICE GUARANTEE

London Dungeon Only Ticket: Online Saver Ticket
Pick an arrival date & time. Book online for the best price guarantee. Plus significantly reduce your waiting time by joining the priority queue with this ticket.

ONLINE SAVER TICKET	DOOR PRICE (not including priority entrance)	WEB PRICE (including priority entrance)	WEB SAVING
Adult (16+)	£24.00	£16.00	£8.00
15 and under	£18.60	£10.00	£8.60

BOOK NOW

1 Using examples from the data provided, explain what is meant by price discrimination. [4]

2 Discuss the benefits of price discrimination to firms such as the London Dungeons. [8]

Answers and quick quizzes online

Online

Examiner's summary

- There are four main market structures for firms selling their output that you need to know for this unit, and they range from many sellers to just one seller. These structures are: perfect competition, monopolistic competition, oligopoly and monopoly.
- There is also a market structure showing the market conditions where there is one powerful buyer, monopsony.
- For each of these market conditions you must be able to show price and output equilibrium points, and be able to show what happens when there are supernormal profits or losses being made.
- You must be able to show what happens when there is an increase or decrease in demand (shift AR and MR) and what happens when there is a change in costs (shift AC and MC if there is a change in variable costs, and shift just AC if there is a change in fixed costs).
- Remember that game theory can be used for your analysis of oligopoly because the firms in this market structure are interdependent.

3 Government intervention

Competition policy

Measures to enhance competition

Revised

Measures aimed at enhancing competition between firms include:

- **Legislation:** the competition authorities can pass laws: for example the Competition Commission has forced the British Airports Authority (BAA) to sell off airports.
- **Privatisation:** this is the selling of public-sector assets to the private sector. The action can force the firm to increase its profitability because it can no longer rely on government subsidy. The competition from other firms might also increase competition, removing x-inefficiency, that is, the organisational slack and unwieldiness that comes when there is no competition.
- **Deregulation:** removing direct controls on firms can allow more competition in markets. The post services in the UK have been subject to large-scale deregulation, which you will notice on your mail as you now see very few letters carrying Royal Mail postage payments. By allowing firms to compete for postal services — meaning the postal worker brings your letters from a large number of suppliers — you have more choice, and hopefully better service and lower prices.
- **Prevention of mergers:** the competition authorities can prevent mergers from happening, or intervene to ensure mergers only occur with certain restrictions in place.
- **Action to prevent abuse of monopoly power:** the regulator looks at aspects of monopoly behaviour, such as the decision by schools to allow only one shop to supply their school uniform. This has been reviewed by the Office of Fair Trading in 2007 and 2012.

Competition policy refers to the set of rules and powers that are used to increase competition within markets. By 2014, competition policy will be in the hands of the Competition and Markets Authority (CMA), which is a merger of the Competition Commission and the anti-monopoly parts of the Office of Fair Trading (OFT). The new body has increased powers to intervene in markets.

Examiner's tip

In most past papers you will see references to the OFT and Competition Commission. You do not need to know their detailed individual powers or history, but you should understand the functions of the competition authority as a whole. You will not need to have up-to-date knowledge of the CMA as there is not enough information available in current text books for you to know.

Now test yourself

Tested

1 Why do governments want to increase competition in markets?

Answers on p. 109

Regulation

Regulation is the means by which governments (or non-government organisations with delegated powers, or quangos) impose restrictions on firms when competition policy is not being used to prevent abuses of market power.

Regulation has been used to act as a surrogate for competition in markets where competition is not easy to achieve. This may be markets with significant monopoly power, e.g. from economies of scale or high barriers to entry such as large amounts of investment in infrastructure. Economists call these natural monopolies. Much industry regulation is imposed on the privatised utilities — gas, water, railways and electricity — firms that were monopolies in the public sector, and when privatised were still going to remain dominant in the markets. This is true for most utilities such as water, gas and electricity markets. However, after BT was privatised in 1984, the telecom industry was heavily regulated, but the industry is largely unregulated now that competitive forces are more strongly in play.

Now test yourself

2 What is the difference between competition policy and regulation?

Answers on p. 109

Tested

Regulation methods

Revised

Price capping

One important method used in the UK is price capping. The regulator can impose a limit on price increases by firms. This is usually done in line with the Retail Price Index (RPI) measure of inflation. Prices are allowed to rise by RPI – X where X is a measure of the amount of efficiency savings the regulator believes the firm can make. Sometimes a value is added to this to allow for investment in the industry, given the letter K. For example water companies currently have an RPI – X + K formula where K allows a price rise to take account of the required increase in investment.

Other forms of regulation

Other forms regulation might take include:

- **Legislation:** the government can pass a law making firms limit carbon emissions or pay taxes in line with their emissions.
- **Monitoring of prices:** in 2012, the prime minister complained that there were 400 different price systems for gas and electricity in the UK. A decision by the gas and electricity regulator, Ofgem, meant that price tariffs had to be simplified and customers would have to be told the best deal they could get. This way, the government could easily assess any abuses of monopoly power.
- **Performance targets for service quality:** for example the Office of Rail Regulation, the regulator of the railways in the UK, measures train punctuality and ensures passengers can get refunds for late arrivals of trains.
- **Licensing and franchises:** the government can control the forms of competition and therefore choice for customers by offering a limited quantity of licences or permission to operate in some markets. The limit on the sale of 4G licences for phones means that there will be some competition, but not so much that it is not profitable for the firms involved to invest.

- **Private-sector involvement in public organisations:** the government pays the costs but market forces are involved in producing goods or services. There are many forms in which this operates. Two important forms for your exam are:
  - Private finance initiative (PFI). This is a form of financing major public projects such as motorway construction or the building of schools and hospitals. The private sector funds the building and maintains the service, and rents or leases the service to the government over a guaranteed period, usually 25–30 years. It was introduced in 1992 in the UK, and has had a significant impact on the government's finances because it can achieve projects today without having to raise the funds in the current period.
  - Contracting out. Many governments use the private sector to provide some services, for example office cleaning, grounds maintenance, leisure services and the management of sports centres, public libraries and arts centres. Since 1988 councils have been required to test their existing arrangements against the best the private sector could offer. Many councils found that they could make substantial savings by contracting out to commercial firms. This is thought to reduce waste and inefficiency in the public sector and to increase the level of competition in the private sector, which leads to lower prices and more choice for consumers.

Examiner's tip

You need to be aware of the importance of the regulatory period. Regulation is imposed on firms for a period of time, and consideration of the length of any control is a very useful tool for evaluation. The longer the regulatory period, the longer the firm can adapt to the controls, and make profits within the parameters set. However if the period is too long, the firm might not be forced to make more efficiency savings, or may be prevented from making profits which would enable it to adapt and grow.

Now test yourself — Tested ☐

3 Does PFI expenditure appear as part of the government's spending and taxation accounts?

Answers on p. 109

Exam practice

Multiple-choice question

1 University College London Hospitals (UCLH) uses the Grafton Hotel at a cost of £120 a night because it is cheaper than the £300 a night cost to the PFI of using hospital care, it was reported in 2010 by the TaxPayers' Alliance. Given the increased costs of PFI to the hospital, which reason best explains why the hospital was built using private finance:

A the government has no experience of building or running hospitals

B the government has a budget surplus

C there is more efficiency in the public sector than the private sector

D it is cheaper for the private sector to borrow than for the public sector

E the government wanted to use its funds elsewhere in the short term [1+3]

Data-response question

Extract: Under one roof — the Competition and Markets Authority

By 2014, the way in which the government intervenes in markets to promote competition and to prevent abuse of market power will be in the hands of the Competition and Markets Authority (CMA). It will combine the full function of the Competition Commission with all the anti-monopoly powers of the Office of Fair Trading (OFT), in the areas which involve looking for collusive behaviour such as price fixing. The OFT will be left with the role of promoting and protecting consumer interests throughout the UK, and ensuring that business practices are fair.

The powers of the CMA will be greatly enhanced. No longer will prosecutors have to prove that firms have acted dishonestly in a collusive agreement, but instead can be prosecuted for not being open in their dealings. The new body will have more experience and the ability to make careful checks, with the funding to attract a high quality of competition lawyers. The body will continue to have the power to force businesses to sell off parts of their firm or to stop selling products even if there is no direct competition law relating to this, but the CMA will no longer need to have to have cases referred to it by the OFT, which can make the process slow and inefficient. It is a merger which is thought to act in the consumer interests, in making the regulatory authority fitter, stronger and able to adapt quickly to decisions by businesses.

An example of the work of the OFT and the Competition Commission is the January 2013 referral of the proposed merger of two NHS foundation trusts located in Poole, Bournemouth and Christchurch to the Competition Commission for an in-depth investigation. The Royal Bournemouth and Christchurch Hospitals NHS Foundation Trust (RBCH) and Poole Hospital NHS Foundation Trust (PHFT) both provide a wide range of hospital and community-based services to patients in Dorset. RBCH has 601 beds on two sites. PHFT has 606 beds, also on two sites. This merger will combine the only two NHS district general hospitals in Bournemouth and Poole, which compete across a range of clinical specialties, in many cases earning income based on the number of patients referred to them in line with the general rule that 'money follows the patient'. The evidence before the OFT is that the merger would combine two trusts that compete closely for GP referrals for many specialties and it is likely that the merger would result in few realistic alternative providers for patients and NHS commissioning groups. As a result, the competition authorities could not dismiss concerns that in several medical specialties the merger might reduce the hospitals' incentives to continue to enhance the quality of those services over the minimum required standards and would result in less choice for commissioners wishing to reorganise services.

Source: www.oft.gov.uk

2 Using examples from the passage, outline the reasons why the government wants to ensure there is competition between firms. **[12]**

3 Using examples from the data and your own knowledge, discuss the likely effectiveness of the new Competition and Markets Authority in the UK. **[16]**

Answers and quick quizzes online

Online

Examiner's tip

In your exam you will have four questions based on some data, with mark bases 4, 8, 12 and 16. However you will be given much more data, and some of the questions will relate to other parts of the specification. You are unlikely to be allocated 40 marks on the basis of one small part of the course, which is why only part of a question paper is given here.

Examiner's summary

- ✔ Governments intervene in markets either to increase competition or to prevent action which would reduce the level of competition.
- ✔ Where increased competition will not improve the welfare of consumers, the government uses regulation, using direct controls to ensure that firms behave in the interests of consumers and other stakeholders.

4 Trade, protectionism and globalisation

World trade

Patterns of trade

Revised

Key factors on patterns of trade include:

- Trade is about three times the level of that in the early 1990s, as a share of global output. The most significant reason for this is the integration of emerging market economies (EEs), which has been increasing rapidly.
- Much of this increased trade is explained by the growth in exports of manufactured goods, especially electronic products and computers. Other reasons include:
  - the growth of global supply chains
  - the increased importance of emerging economies as trading partners
  - the fragmentation of the production processes along vertical trading chains which are spread across many countries. Consequently, intermediate goods are transferred between several countries before they become final goods

Figure 4.1 illustrates the share of selected countries' world trade over the last 30 years and how this is expected to change. This may be explained by the factors above and also by considering changes in comparative advantage, which is described in the following section.

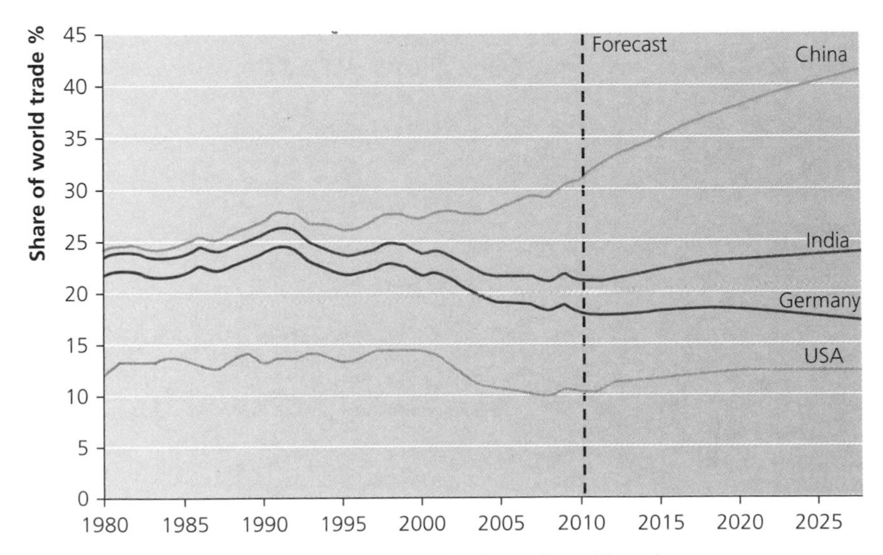

Figure 4.1 USA, Germany, China and India's share of world trade 1980–2025 (Source: Oxford Economics)

Now test yourself

1 Suggest three reasons why China's share of world trade has increased and is expected to increase further.

Answers on p. 109

Tested

The law of comparative advantage

Patterns of trade may be explained by the law of **comparative advantage**. A country has comparative advantage if it can produce a good with a lower opportunity cost than that of another country. This means that trade between the two nations can be beneficial to both if each specialises in the production of a good with lower relative opportunity cost.

One country has **comparative advantage** over another in the production of a good if it can produce it at a lower opportunity cost.

Examiner's tip

The law of comparative advantage is not only fundamental to an explanation of international trade, but it also applies to specialisation and the division of labour.

Assumptions

Revised

Assumptions underlying the law of comparative advantage include:

- Constant returns to scale. This implies that an increase in the factors of production or the scale of production leads to an exactly proportionate increase in output. This would imply that the production possibility frontiers are drawn as straight lines.
- No transport costs.
- No barriers to international trade, i.e. there are no restrictions on trade between countries.
- Perfect mobility of factors of production between different uses.
- Externalities are ignored. For example, external costs associated with transporting goods between countries are not considered.

Examiner's tip

Obviously, these assumptions are restrictive; they may be used in evaluating the law of comparative advantage.

Absolute advantage

Revised

Absolute advantage implies that a country can produce more of one product than another country. Figure 4.2 illustrates a situation in which country A has an absolute advantage in the production of maize and country B has an absolute advantage in the production of smart phones.

A country is said to have an **absolute advantage** in its production if it can produce more of a product than another country

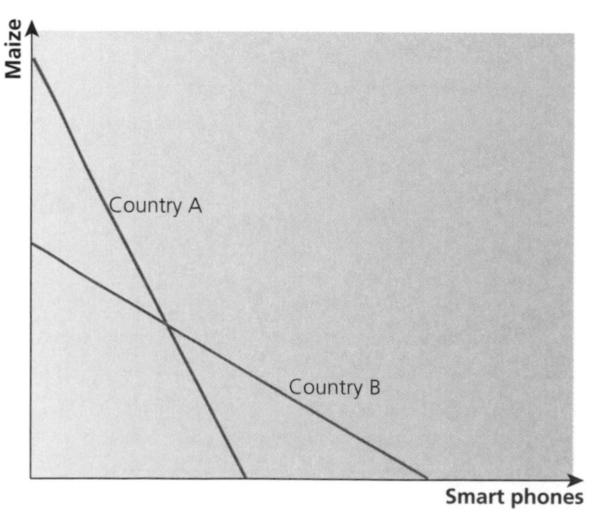

Figure 4.2 Country A has an absolute advantage in maize and country B has an absolute advantage in smart phones

In this case, it is clear that each country could benefit by specialising in the product in which it has an absolute advantage.

Typical mistake

Using Figure 4.2 to explain comparative advantage. Comparative advantage should be explained and illustrated using Figure 4.3.

Comparative advantage

Revised

David Ricardo demonstrated that even if one country had an absolute advantage in the production of both products, it could still benefit from specialisation and trade by concentrating on production of the product in which it had a comparative advantage, i.e. in which it was relatively more efficient. The crucial requirement is that there must be a difference in the opportunity cost of producing the products.

Comparative advantage illustrated diagrammatically

Figure 4.3 illustrates this principle:

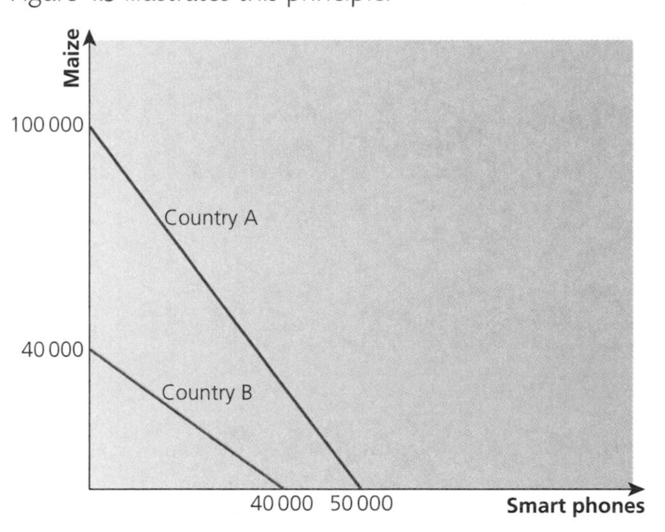

Figure 4.3 Country A has an absolute advantage in both products

Comparative advantage illustrated numerically

The following tables illustrate this principle.

Suppose countries A and B both produce two products, maize and smart phones. They can both produce the following amounts of these products with the same quantity of resources:

Country	Maize (kg)	Smart phones
A	100 000 *or*	50 000
B	40 000 *or*	40 000

Clearly, country A has an absolute advantage in the production of both maize and smart phones. If each country devotes half its resources to the production of each product then output would be as follows:

Country	Maize (kg)	Smart phones
A	50 000	25 000
B	20 000	20 000
Total	70 000 *and*	45 000

To determine whether trade will be worthwhile, the **opportunity costs** must be calculated:

Country	Opportunity cost of producing 1 kg of maize	Opportunity cost of producing 1 smart phone
A	½	2
B	1	1

From the table it can be seen that country A has a comparative advantage in maize (because the opportunity cost is lower) while country B has a comparative advantage in smart phones.

For trade to be beneficial, the **terms of trade** must lie between the opportunity cost ratios. In this case, the terms of trade must lie between 1 and 2 kg of maize for 1 smart phone.

The terms of trade are measured as follows:

$$\frac{\text{index of export prices}}{\text{index of import prices}} \times 100$$

You should note that if the opportunity costs were the same, then there would be no benefit from specialisation and trade.

Terms of trade: measures the average price of a country's exports relative to the average price of its imports.

Examiner's tip

Note that the concept of terms of trade is also relevant when discussing primary product dependency in developing countries.

Now test yourself Tested

2 What is the difference between absolute advantage and comparative advantage?

Answers on p. 109

Criticisms of the law of comparative advantage

Revised

Despite widespread acceptance of the law of comparative advantage among economists and support for the benefits of free trade, various criticisms can be made:

- Free trade is not necessarily fair trade (i.e. the rich countries might exert their **monopsony** power to force producers in developing countries to accept very low prices).
- The law of comparative advantage is based on unrealistic assumptions such as constant costs of production, zero transport costs and no barriers to trade.

Monopsony refers to a sole buyer of a product or service. In this case 'monopsony power' refers to the buying power of rich developed countries over developing countries which supply the raw materials, components and products.

The Heckscher-Ohlin Model

Revised

Ricardo's theory of comparative advantage was further developed in what has become known as the Heckscher-Ohlin model. This model predicts that patterns of production and trade are based on the factor endowments of a trading region. This model suggests that countries will specialise in the production and export of goods which use resources which are in abundant supply and import products which use its scarce resources.

Free trade

Advantages of free trade

Revised

The advantages of free trade are:

- **Higher living standards:** the law of comparative advantage illustrates an important benefit of free trade, namely, that world output will increase. This implies that consumers will benefit from higher living standards.

- **Lower prices:** consumers will benefit from imported goods which have been produced more efficiently and whose price is therefore lower, resulting in a higher **consumers' surplus**.
- **Increased choice:** consumers are able to purchase products not available in their countries and will benefit from a greater range of a particular product, e.g. cars.
- **Economies of scale:** firms may benefit because there may be a larger market for their products, enabling them to expand output. Producing a larger amount of goods might enable firms to benefit from economies of scale causing a fall in long-run average costs which could result in higher profits.

Consumers' surplus refers to the difference between consumers' willingness to pay and what they have to pay.

Examiner's tip

In considering the advantages of international trade, it is important to refer to theory e.g. the law of comparative advantage.

The role of the World Trade Organization (WTO)

Revised

The key roles of the WTO and its forerunner, the General Agreement on Tariffs and Trade (GATT), are:

- To promote free trade: this is achieved through various rounds of talks. However, the Doha Round, which was started in November 2001, was still not concluded by 2012.
- To settle trade disputes between member countries.
- Following the entry of Russia to the WTO in 2012, there are now 188 members. Many would argue that these organisations have played a key role in the closer integration of the world economy.

Disadvantages of free trade

Revised

Despite the advantages of free trade outlined above, there are some potential problems for individual countries including:

- A deficit on the **trade in goods and services balance**: if a country's goods and services are uncompetitive then imports will increase relative to exports and there will be a deterioration in its trade in goods and services balance.
- Danger of **dumping**: firms in countries with surpluses of goods might 'dump' them on other countries, which would undermine local producers, perhaps causing them to go bankrupt. In the long run, the country could then become dependent on imports.
- Increased unemployment in some countries: both the above factors could result in a higher rate of unemployment for a particular country.
- Increased risk of disruption resulting from problems in the global economy; for example, the countries which suffered the sharpest downturn following the financial crisis of 2008 were those heavily dependent on exports.
- Unbalanced development: international specialisation based on free trade means that only those industries in which the country has a comparative advantage will be developed while others will remain undeveloped. In other words, there will be **sectoral imbalance** which may restrict the overall rate of economic growth.
- Global **monopolies**: free trade enables transnational companies (TNCs) to gain monopoly power. These TNCs might exploit consumers by restricting output, causing an increase in price.

Trade in goods and services balance refers to the value of exports minus the value of imports.

Dumping occurs when a product is sold in a foreign country for less than the cost of making the product. Under the rules of the WTO, this practice is illegal.

Sectoral imbalance refers to an imbalance in the three main sectors of the economy — primary, secondary and tertiary sectors.

Monopolies are sole suppliers of a product.

- Developing countries may face problems for a variety of reasons including:
  - infant industries may be unable to compete and may go out of business
  - monopsony power of firms in developed economies might force producers in developing countries to accept low prices for their products
  - countries dependent on primary products may face declining terms of trade

The above reasons provide the basis of the rationale for protectionist policies designed to limit free trade between countries.

Now test yourself Tested

3 From the perspective of consumers and workers, identify two advantages and two disadvantages of free trade.

4 From the perspective of a firm, identify two advantages and two disadvantages of free trade.

Answers on p. 110

Protectionism

Types of trade barriers

Revised

Examples of trade barriers are shown in Figure 4.4.

Protectionism means methods of restricting free trade.

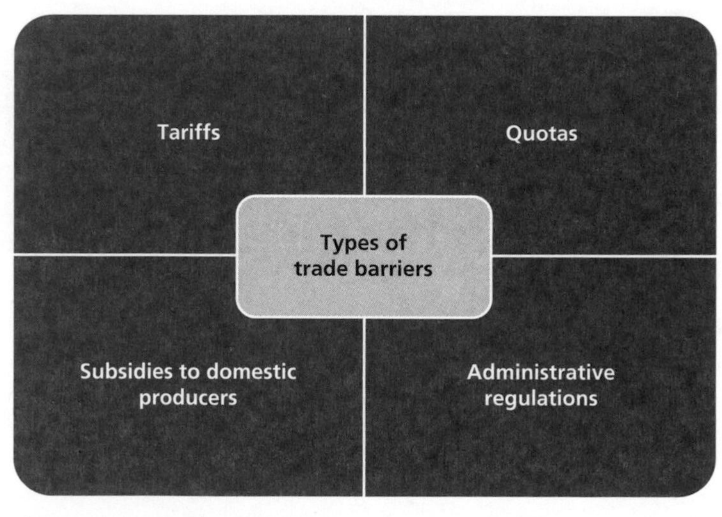

Figure 4.4 Types of trade barriers

Tariffs and customs duties

Tariffs and customs duties are taxes placed on imports that artificially raise the price of imported goods. This is designed to make the domestically produced goods more attractive to consumers. Figure 4.5 shows the impact of a tariff on a particular product on both domestic output and on the level of imports.

Tariffs are taxes on imported goods.

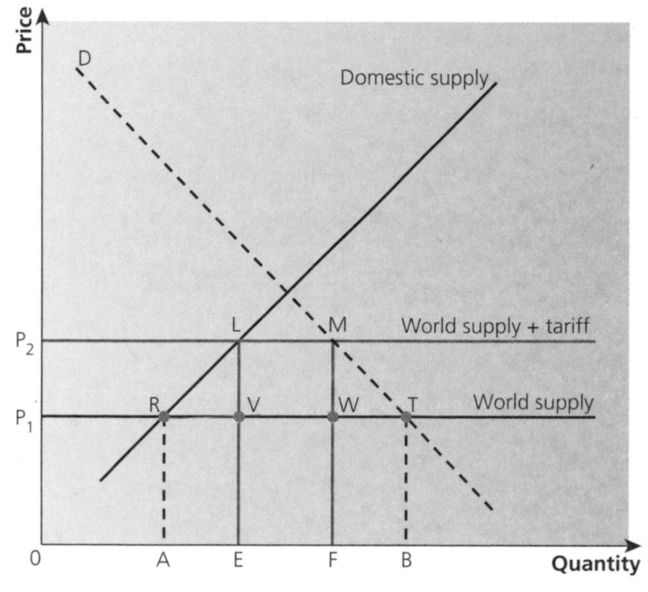

Figure 4.5 The effects of a tariff on cars

The table below summarises the effects of the tariff with reference to Figure 4.5.

	Before tariff is imposed	After tariff is imposed
Price paid by consumers	P_1	P_2
Domestic output	0A	0E
Imports	AB	EF
Tax revenue	Zero	LMVW
Net welfare loss	Zero	RLV and WMT

Quotas

Quotas are limits on the physical quantity of a product which may be imported. As with tariffs the price to domestic consumers will increase and domestic output will rise.

Quotas are limits on the quantity of a product imported.

Subsidies to domestic producers

Subsidies are government grants to firms which reduce costs of production, so causing the supply curve of domestic producers to shift to the right. Figure 4.6 illustrates the impact of subsidies.

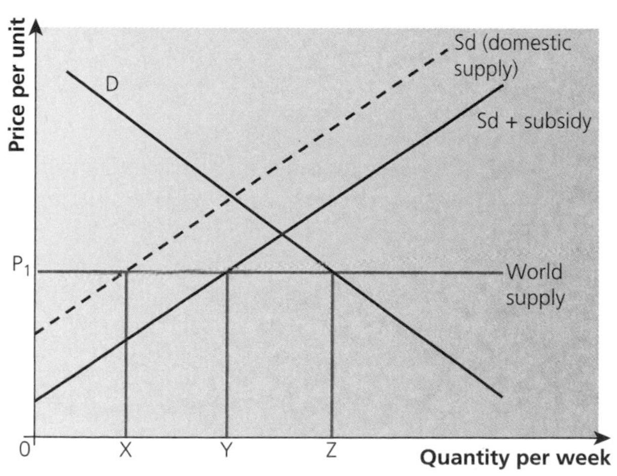

Figure 4.6 The effect of a subsidy

The effects of a subsidy to domestic producers are summarised in the table below.

	Before subsidy	After subsidy
Price paid by consumers	P_1	P_1
Domestic output	0X	0Y
Imports	XY	YZ

It can be seen that the effect on imports is similar to that of tariffs but in this case the price does not change and the government does not receive any tax revenue. Indeed, this method involves public expenditure to finance the subsidies to domestic producers.

Examiner's tip

This analysis is essentially the same as that for subsidies covered in Unit 1. However, it is given a global context by including world supply.

Administrative regulations

Given that GATT and WTO agreements have reduced tariffs, countries have resorted to a wide range of alternative methods to restrict imports. These include:

- health and safety regulations
- environmental regulations
- labelling of products
- bureaucracy, e.g. requiring importers to complete a vast number of forms

All these may raise the cost of imports and/or deter foreign companies from attempting to export goods to that country.

Now test yourself Tested

5 Identify two differences in the effects of a tariff and a subsidy to domestic producers.

Answers on p. 110

The disadvantages of protectionism

Revised

Protectionism has serious disadvantages:

- It may cause retaliation, i.e. other countries might impose protectionist measures in response to a country which has introduced tariffs.
- It results in inefficiency as domestic firms face less competition and have less incentive to produce at lowest average cost.
- It distorts comparative advantage. This means that specialisation is reduced resulting in lower output.
- Consumer welfare is reduced. For example, tariffs and quotas result in higher prices and a reduction in consumers' surplus. Further, consumer choice is likely to be restricted.

Examiner's tip

Understanding the disadvantages of protectionism can help in evaluating the benefits of free trade.

Trading blocs

What is a trading bloc?

Revised

A **trading bloc** is a group of countries usually within a geographical region designed to significantly reduce or remove trade barriers within member countries. The number and size of trading blocs has increased significantly over the last 50 years. The world is now increasingly divided

Trading blocs are groups of countries that agree to reduce or eliminate trade barriers between themselves.

into trading blocs, most of which are in specific geographical regions. For example, the East African Community (EAC), the Common Market for Eastern and Southern Africa (COMESA), and the Southern African Development Community (SADC) which aims to create a free market of 525 million people with an output of $1 trillion when they unite in 2014.

Further examples of trading blocs include:

- the European Union (EU)
- the North American Free Trade Agreement (NAFTA)
- the Common Market of the South (MERCOSUR), whose the full members are Argentina, Brazil, Paraguay, Uruguay and, from 2012, Venezuela
- the Central American Common Market (CACM)
- the Association of Southeast Asian Nations (ASEAN)

Typical mistake

The term 'trading bloc' is sometimes assumed to mean blocks or restrictions on trade: this is incorrect!

Examiner's tip

It is useful to know examples of trading blocs so you can include these in your answers.

Types of trading blocs

Revised

Trading blocs take several forms which include:

- **Free trade areas:** as the term suggests, in these trading blocs trade barriers are removed between member countries but each member can impose trade restrictions on non-members.
- **Customs unions:** there is free trade between member countries combined with a common external tariff on goods from countries outside the customs union, i.e. a tax is imposed at an agreed rate on goods imported from non-member countries.
- **Common markets:** these have the same characteristics as customs unions but include the added dimension of the free movement of factors of production between member countries. Of these resources, labour tends to be the most mobile.
- **Monetary unions:** these are customs unions which adopt a common currency.

Typical mistake

It is incorrect to assume that all trading blocs have the same characteristics. As may be seen from the list above, there are many forms of trading blocs.

Trading blocs and the WTO

Revised

The goal of the WTO is to promote free trade. Although trading blocs are characterised by free trade between member countries, they restrict trade with non-member countries. Some would infer that trading blocs conflict with the aims of the WTO. However, the WTO has found it difficult to secure agreement on reducing trade barriers between members and, as has been noted, both the number and size of trading blocs has been increasing, so it may be argued that they have played an important role in promoting free trade.

Now test yourself

Tested

6 What is the theoretical basis for the World Trade Organization?
7 Distinguish between trade creation and trade diversion.

Answers on p. 110

Globalisation

What is globalisation?

Revised

Globalisation refers to the increased economic integration between countries. There are many ways in which globalisation manifests itself including:

- **Increased trade as a proportion of GDP:** since 1960, trade as a percentage of GDP has increased from less than 25% to over 57%, demonstrating clearly the increased economic integration of the world economy. Figure 4.7 shows the growth of exports as a proportion of GDP.

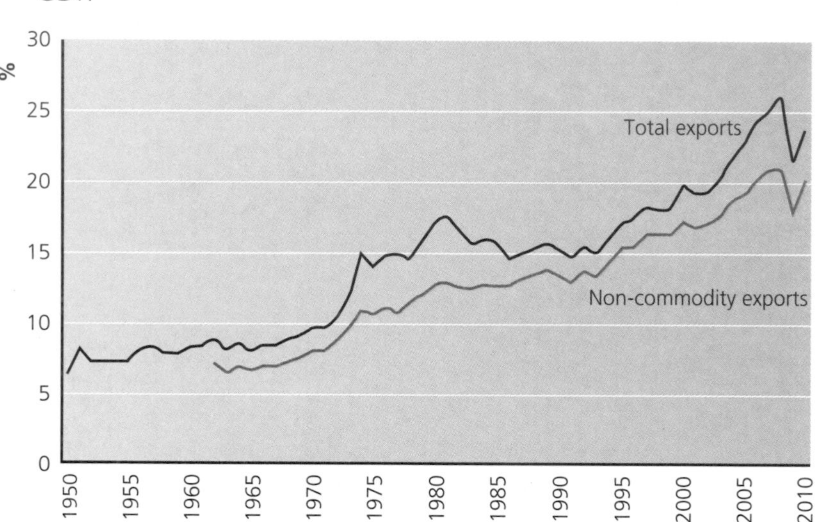

Figure 4.7 World exports as a percentage of GDP (Source: IMF)

- **Increased foreign direct investment (FDI):** FDI has meant that many manufacturing plants have moved from developed countries to low-wage developing economies.
- **Increased capital flows between countries: capital flows** relate to money flowing into and out of the stock and bond markets of countries around the world, as well as factors such as real estate and cross-border mergers and acquisitions. These capital flows have increased as cross-border acquisitions and mergers of companies have grown in different countries.
- **Increased movement of labour between countries:** free movement of labour, for example between members of a common market, is a further factor which has contributed to globalisation.

Economist Peter Jay defines **globalisation** as 'the ability to produce any good or service anywhere in the world, using raw materials, components, capital and technology from anywhere, sell the resulting output anywhere and place the profits anywhere'.

Examiner's tip

Although globalisation has social and cultural dimensions, it is important to focus your exam answers on its economic implications.

Capital flows refer to all the money moving between countries as a consequence of investment flows into and out of countries around the world.

Now test yourself

Tested

8 Suggest three reasons why trade between countries might continue to increase in the next 20 years.

Answers on p. 110

Examiner's tip

Although globalisation may be interpreted very broadly, you should focus on its economic aspects when answering questions in economics exams.

Causes of globalisation

Revised

Globalisation is not a new phenomenon but the pace of globalisation has increased significantly in the last 40 years. However, the financial crisis of

2008 and subsequent turmoil in the world economy restricted further global integration. Causes of globalisation include the following:

- **Decrease in the cost of transport.** Containerisation has meant that vast quantities can be transported by sea and road at very low average cost as a result of the benefits of economies of scale.
- **Decrease in cost of communications.** Researchers at the Boston Consulting Group (BCG) estimated that, in 2010, the internet economy was worth £121 billion to the UK economy, a bigger share than for any of the other G20 major countries. They predict it will continue to expand at a rate of 11% per year, reaching a total value of £221 billion by 2016. Super-fast broadband and 4G technology will play a significant role in this growth.
- **Reduction in world trade barriers.** GATT and its successor, the WTO, have brought about significant reductions in trade barriers. As more countries have become members, the reduction in barriers has had a significant impact on the growth in world trade. A recent addition to the WTO is Russia who became a member in 2012.
- **The opening up of China and the collapse of communism in Eastern Europe.** The introduction of economic reforms in China since the late 1970s has resulted in spectacular rates of economic growth not least because of the increase in foreign investment, which has resulted in China becoming a major manufacturing nation. The period 1989–91 saw the collapse of the Soviet bloc and the introduction of various forms of market economy. This resulted in these countries becoming more closely integrated into the world economy.
- **Growth of trading blocs.** Trading blocs (see definition in key term box on page 48) help to promote globalisation because there is free trade between member countries. There has been a growth in the number and size of trading blocs since the Second World War. Examples include NAFTA; MERCOSUR; ASEAN: EU; SADC; and ECOWAS.
- **Increased importance of transnational companies.** TNCs have undertaken much FDI, which frequently involves moving manufacturing to a country where production costs are lower — a practice known as **offshoring**.

Offshoring refers to companies transferring manufacturing to a different country.

Now test yourself Tested ☐

9 Why is the internet a significant cause of globalisation?

Answers on p. 110

Benefits of globalisation

Revised ☐

It is argued that the globalisation which has occurred over the last 40 years has brought a variety of benefits. These include the following:

- **Higher living standards.** With lower trade barriers and increased trade, countries can specialise in producing goods in which they have a comparative advantage. This results in higher world output so enabling an increase in living standards.

- **Economies of scale.** Firms will be producing on a larger scale and so will benefit from falling long-run average costs as a result of economies of scale.
- **Lower prices.** Globalisation has meant that manufacturing has moved to countries where the costs of production (especially labour) are lowest. This has resulted in lower real prices for many goods, especially clothes and electronic equipment. Lower prices have resulted in an increase in consumers' surplus.
- **Increased consumer choice.** The increase in world trade has resulted in a wider variety of goods being available in countries.
- **Reduction in absolute poverty in developing countries.** As developing countries have become more closely integrated into the world economy, they have experienced an increase in their real GDPs which has helped to reduce the number of people living in **absolute poverty**.
- **Increased tax revenues.** As GDP increases, governments will receive increased tax revenues from individuals and companies which they can then use for expenditure on public services such as health and education or for infrastructure.
- **Technology transfer.** When TNCs invest in other countries they are likely to bring modern technology with them. Domestic firms might benefit from adopting this technology, which should result in increased productivity.
- **New managerial techniques.** Similarly, TNCs are likely to introduce modern managerial techniques designed to increase productivity.

Absolute poverty refers to people who have insufficient resources to meet basic human needs such as water, food, clothing and shelter. (See also pages 78–9.)

Examiner's tip

- Notice that some of the benefits of globalisation are the same as those of free trade.
- Remember that this is a synoptic unit so it is important to use concepts introduced in previous units, such as standard of living, economies of scale and consumers' surplus.

Costs of globalisation

Revised

Despite the above advantages, there are several costs associated with globalisation including the following:

- **Negative externalities resulting from increased production and trade.** Negative externalities can result from increased production and trade. For example, with increased trade there will be increased road and air transport which involves carbon dioxide emissions, so causing pollution.
- **Over-dependence on imports.** A country which does not have a competitive advantage may come to rely increasingly on imports, which would cause deterioration in the current account of the balance of payments.
- **Risk of contagion is increased.** Increased integration of countries into the world economy makes them more susceptible to global economic crises. For example, those countries heavily dependent on exports were particularly affected by the global financial crisis in 2008.
- **Increased inequality.** It is argued that globalisation has resulted in increased inequality within countries. One reason for this is that the demand for unskilled labour has decreased in developed countries, so increasing the earnings gap between the highest-paid and lowest-paid workers.

Negative externalities are costs to third parties who are not directly involved in a transaction.

- **Exploitation of labour.** TNCs might exploit workers in developing countries by paying low wages for long working hours. Further, some TNCs have been accused of employing child labour.
- **Exploitation of resources.** Some countries have invested aggressively in developing countries that are rich in natural resources in order to secure future supplies of resources. For example, China has invested in copper mines in Zambia.
- **Tax avoidance.** Some TNCs engage in **transfer pricing** to minimise their tax burden in countries with relatively high corporate taxes.

Transfer pricing refers to the price that has been charged by one part of a company for products and services it provides to another part of the same company. This system enables TNCs to declare profits in the country in which corporation tax is lowest.

Exam practice

Essay questions

1 **(a)** Assess the causes of globalisation in recent years. [20]

(b) Evaluate the benefits of globalisation. [30]

2 Assess the economic effects of trading blocs on the global economy. [20]

Data-response question

Extract: World trade since 2008

From the end of the Second World War until 2008 world trade expanded significantly. However, the financial crisis and recession in many developed countries led to deglobalisation, which manifested itself in a fall in world trade, lower foreign direct investment and a lower level of short-run money flows between countries.

Countries whose exports were a large proportion of GDP were particularly affected. For example, Taiwan's exports were 60% of its GDP while Singapore's were a staggering 186% of GDP. Developed countries such as Germany and Japan, which exported a large quantity of capital goods and electronic products, were also affected by the crisis. Inevitably, the economic growth rates in these countries fell significantly. However, once the worst of the crisis was over, they recovered quickly.

During the economic downturn and subsequently, protectionism has increased in the form of both tariffs, and subsidies to domestic producers who have faced difficulties. One reason was that many countries were facing pressure from their electorates because unemployment levels were increasing rapidly.

A further problem was that some countries, including developing countries, that had developed tourism, faced particular difficulties because the financial crisis resulted in a sharp downturn in tourist numbers, especially from developed countries to exotic destinations such as Barbados, Kenya and the Far East.

3 **(a)** Explain the key features of globalisation. [5]

(b) With reference to the information provided and your own knowledge, analyse two possible reasons for deglobalisation. [8]

(c) In the light of the information provided, assess the disadvantages for a country which is heavily dependent on tourism. [12]

(d) Evaluate the likely economic effects of an increase in protectionism on the world economy. [15]

Answers and quick quizzes online

Online

Examiner's summary

You should have an understanding of:

- ✔ The law of comparative advantage.
- ✔ Advantages of trade.
- ✔ The World Trade Organization.
- ✔ Disadvantages of trade.
- ✔ Trading blocs.
- ✔ Types of protection: tariffs, quotas, subsidies to domestic producers.
- ✔ Administrative regulations.
- ✔ Disadvantages of protectionism.
- ✔ Globalisation: meaning; causes; costs and benefits.

5 The balance of payments, exchange rates and international competitiveness

The balance of payments

The **balance of payments** is a record of all financial transactions between one country and those in the rest of the world.

There are two main elements of the balance of payments accounts: the current account and the financial account.

The **balance of payments** is a set of accounts showing one country's financial transactions with other countries.

The current account

Revised

The **current account** consists of several elements, the most important of which are:

- **The trade in goods balance:** value of goods exported minus value of goods imported.
- **The trade in services balance:** value of services exported minus value of services imported.
- **Investment income:** income earned from assets owned overseas minus income paid to foreigners for assets owned in the UK.
- **Current transfers:** payments received from foreign institutions (e.g. the EU) minus payments paid abroad (e.g. to the EU or food aid to developing countries).

The sum of the above items will give the current account.

If the result is negative there is said to be a deficit on the current account of the balance of payments or simply a **current account deficit**.

If the result is positive there is said to be a surplus on the current account of the balance of payments or simply a **current account surplus**.

The **current account** of the balance of payments shows a country's day-to-day transactions with other countries.

A **current account deficit** occurs when the value of goods and services imported is greater than the value of goods and services exported.

A **current account surplus** occurs when the value of goods and services exported is greater than the value of goods and services imported.

The capital and financial accounts

Revised

This part of the accounts is concerned with changes of ownership of the UK's foreign financial assets and liabilities. It comprises several elements, the most important of which are:

- foreign direct investment (investment by foreign companies into the UK minus investment by UK companies abroad)
- portfolio investment in shares and bonds (purchase of UK shares and bonds by foreigners minus purchase of foreign shares and bonds by UK citizens)
- short-term capital flows, often referred to as hot-money flows (money flows into the UK minus flows out of the UK to other countries)
- changes in foreign currency reserves

The **capital and financial accounts** of the balance of payments show long-term investments and short-term capital flows.

The UK usually enjoys a surplus on this part of the balance of payments, not least because it has been very successful in attracting foreign direct investment.

The UK's current account

Revised

Figure 5.1 shows the UK's trade in goods balance, the trade in services balance and the current account balance:

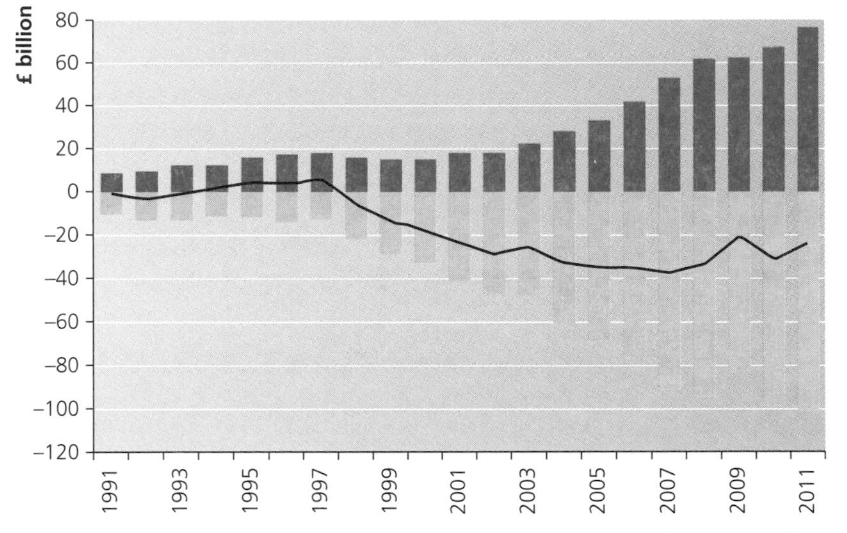

Figure 5.1 The UK's current account of the balance of payments (Source: ONS)

It can be seen from Figure 5.1 that since 1991 the UK has experienced a continuous deficit on its trade in goods balance and a continuous surplus on its balance of trade in services. The overall current account has been in deficit since the late 1990s.

Reasons for the UK's current account deficit

- The UK's relatively low productivity has meant that its goods and services have not been competitive.
- This has been associated with the relocation of many manufacturing industries from the UK to countries where labour costs are significantly lower, such as China and Eastern Europe. However, as labour costs and transport costs have been increasing more recently, some firms have returned to the UK.
- The high value of sterling between 1996 and 2008 also contributed to a loss of competitiveness.
- Similarly, continuous economic growth between 1992 and 2008 contributed to the deficit because the UK has a high marginal propensity to import.
- Despite the 27% depreciation in the value of sterling in 2008–09, there has not been a significant improvement in the current account, largely because of the economic slowdown in the EU, which buys about 45% of UK exports.

Examiner's tip

Remember that the balance of payments is concerned with external balance (related to trade and financial transactions between countries) whereas the budget balance relates to internal balance (the relationship between government expenditure and tax revenues).

Examiner's tip

The balance of payments is a set of accounts and so it must balance each year. Therefore, if there is a current account deficit, there must be a corresponding surplus on the capital and financial account. If necessary, this could be achieved by drawing on reserves of gold and foreign currency or from loans from abroad, e.g. from the International Monetary Fund (IMF).

Now test yourself Tested

1. For each of the following, state whether they would be part of the current account or financial account and whether they would have a positive or negative impact on the UK's balance of payments:
   (a) UK sells JCBs to Brazil.
   (b) UK citizen takes a holiday in Bali.
   (c) Investment by Toyota into an extension of its UK car factory.
   (d) Wine imported into the UK from Chile.
   (e) Dividends paid to US shareholders of Kraft as a result of profits made by Cadbury, its UK subsidiary.
2. Which of the following is likely to cause an improvement in the UK's trade in goods balance?
   (a) An increase in real incomes of the UK's major trading partners.
   (b) An increase in the UK's inflation rate.
   (c) A decrease in the UK's productivity rate.
   (d) An increase in the UK's income tax rates.

Answers on p. 110

Significance of a current account deficit

Revised

A persistent current account deficit may be undesirable:

- if it indicates that the country's goods and services are uncompetitive
- in turn, this may result in an increasing rate of unemployment
- ultimately, the country may be forced to borrow foreign currency from other countries or from the IMF if its reserves fall too low
- further, under a system of floating exchange rates, a persistent current account deficit could result in a sudden depreciation of the exchange rate

However, a current account deficit may not be regarded as a major problem if:

- it is caused by imports of capital goods
- it is only a short-run problem
- it can be financed easily by inflows into the financial account

Measures to reduce a current account deficit

Revised

When considering how a country might reduce its current account deficit, the context is of key importance. For example, countries that are part of the Eurozone cannot unilaterally raise tariffs or give subsidies to firms unless they are acting under an EU agreement. Further, countries whose currencies are floating cannot 'devalue' their currencies although they might engineer a depreciation through cutting interest rates. (The implications of devaluation and depreciation will be considered in the section on exchange rates on pages 58–60.)

Consequently, the policies available to a government to increase competitiveness may be quite limited.

The following supply-side policies could be used:

- **Cut in corporation tax:** for example, the UK is cutting its corporation tax from 28% in 2010 to 21% in 2014. The aim is to promote enterprise and provide incentives for firms to increase investment, although this may also be achieved by tax breaks to companies who use profits for investment. In turn, this could increase productivity and so make UK goods more competitive.
- **Improved infrastructure:** for instance, new schemes such as Crossrail and the second Forth Road Bridge in Scotland. In 2012, the UK government offered guarantees designed to underwrite the financing for £40 billion of stalled projects within the National Infrastructure Plan. All such measures would help to improve the supply side of the economy.
- **Superfast broadband:** this could help to boost competitiveness.
- **Training and education:** improved training schemes and improvements in education could lead to increased productivity and also increase the occupational mobility of labour.
- **Reduction in regulation and red tape:** measures such as a reduction in bureaucracy, environmental regulations and health and safety requirements might also help to reduce costs of firms.
- **Modern apprenticeships:** these are designed to give people skills in a particular occupation and so help to increase employability as well as increasing the productivity of the workforce.
- **Reduction in employers' national insurance contributions:** this measure would reduce costs of production and so help to improve competitiveness.
- **Improved childcare provision:** typically, Nordic countries have much better and cheaper childcare arrangements than the UK. It is estimated that if these were adopted in the UK, then more than a million more women would join the workforce.

Other policy measures could also help to reduce a current account deficit. For example, expenditure-reducing policies such as a deflationary fiscal policy may be employed. These include increasing taxes and/or reducing public expenditure, the effect of which would be to reduce disposable income and so reduce imports.

Now test yourself Tested

3 Explain how demand-side policies might be used to reduce a current account deficit.

Answers on p. 110

Global imbalances

Revised

These refer to the fact that some countries have been running persistent and large current account deficits, such as the USA and the UK, while others have been running persistent and large current account surpluses, for instance China, Germany and many oil-exporting countries. These differences in current accounts are often associated with differences in savings ratios. For example, China's savings ratio is around 50%, considerably higher than those of the USA and UK. Some have argued that, since the balance of payments must always balance, these imbalances are insignificant. However, in the aftermath of the global financial crisis, some economists argue that huge current account deficits are unsustainable and can lead to significant fluctuations in the value of currencies, which limit the growth of world trade and should, therefore, be addressed.

Figure 5.2 shows that, since the financial crisis of 2008, global imbalances have decreased.

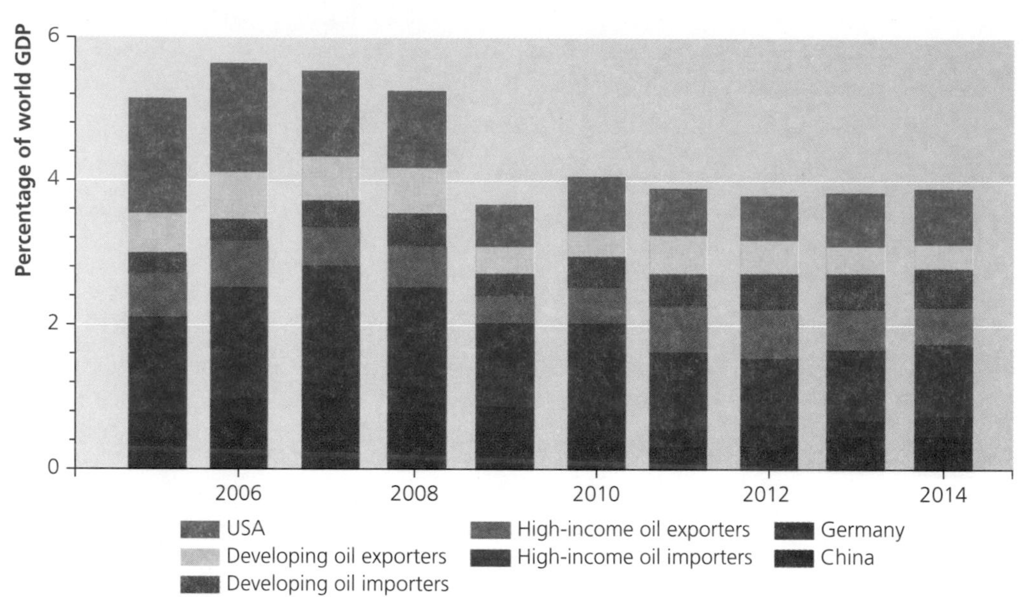

Figure 5.2 Global imbalances as a percentage of global GDP (Source: World Bank)

Exchange rates

The exchange rate is the rate at which one currency exchanges for another or the value of one currency in relation to other currencies. One currency may also be valued against a basket of other currencies weighted according to their relative importance in world trade. This is called the **trade-weighted index**.

Factors influencing exchange rates

Revised

There are a range of factors which can influence the value of a currency in relation to others, including the following:

- **Relative interest rates:** if a country has much higher interest rates than others this may attract money into its banks from abroad because of the prospect of gaining a higher return. This creates an increased demand for the currency so causing its value to rise.
- **Relative inflation rates:** if a country has a higher inflation rate than its competitors, then its purchasing power will fall relative to its competitors and, in the long term, it is likely that its exchange rate will fall. This may be explained in terms of **purchasing power parity** theory.
- **Current account balance:** if a country is running a persistent current account deficit it implies that the supply of its currency is increasing

Purchasing power parity theory states that the exchange rate between one country and another is in equilibrium when their domestic purchasing powers at that exchange rate are the same.

relative to the demand for it, resulting in a depreciation in its currency. However, financial flows between countries relating to trade are now much less significant than currency flows relating to other transactions.

- **Foreign direct investment (FDI):** a country which is a net recipient of FDI will experience an increased demand for its currency so causing its value to appreciate.
- **Speculation:** speculation arises for a number of reasons, e.g. expected state of the economy, an expected change in interest rates or fears about a rising rate of inflation in the future.

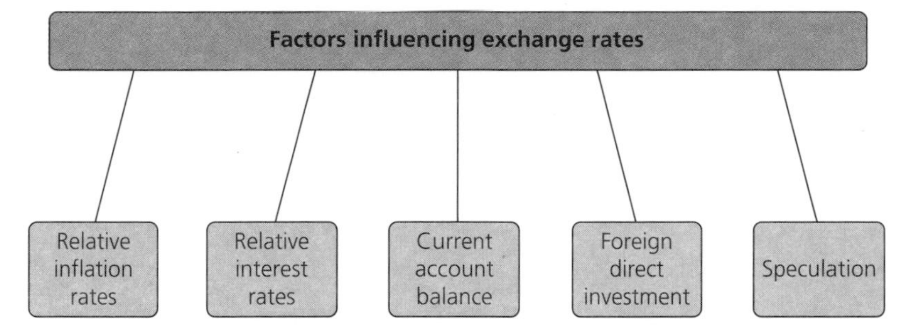

Figure 5.3 Factors influencing exchange rates

Effects of a depreciation in the value of a currency

Revised

This would cause:

- A decrease in the foreign currency price of a country's exports.
- An increase in the domestic price of its imports.

These two factors would cause an increase in the competitiveness of the country's goods and services and so should help to improve the current account of the country's balance of payments.

Apart from the effects on the balance of payments, there are broader impacts on the economy:

- In terms of aggregate demand/aggregate supply analysis, this should lead to an increase in aggregate demand so causing a rise in real output and an increase in the price level.
- Further, the increased price of imported commodities and raw materials would cause an increase in costs of production, so leading to cost–push inflation.
- The rise in real output should help to reduce unemployment.

However, these changes may not occur immediately, if at all, as explained below.

The Marshall–Lerner condition

Revised

This states that the current account of the balance of payments will only improve if the sum of the price elasticities of demand for exports and imports is greater than 1. Therefore, if this condition is not fulfilled, a depreciation in the currency would cause the current account deficit to increase.

The J-curve effect

Revised

The effects of a depreciation may be different in the short run from the effects in the long run. In the short run, a depreciation might cause a deterioration in the current account of the balance of payments because:

- the demand for imports might be price inelastic if firms have stocks or if they are tied into contracts
- the demand for exports might be price inelastic because consumers take time to adjust to the new, lower prices

The **J-curve effect** describes the difference in the short-run and long-run effects of a depreciation in the exchange rate of a country's economy.

Consequently, it would only be in the long run when these factors are no longer relevant that there would be an improvement in the current account of the balance of payments. This difference in short-run and long-run effects is often referred to as the **J-curve effect** and is illustrated in Figure 5.4.

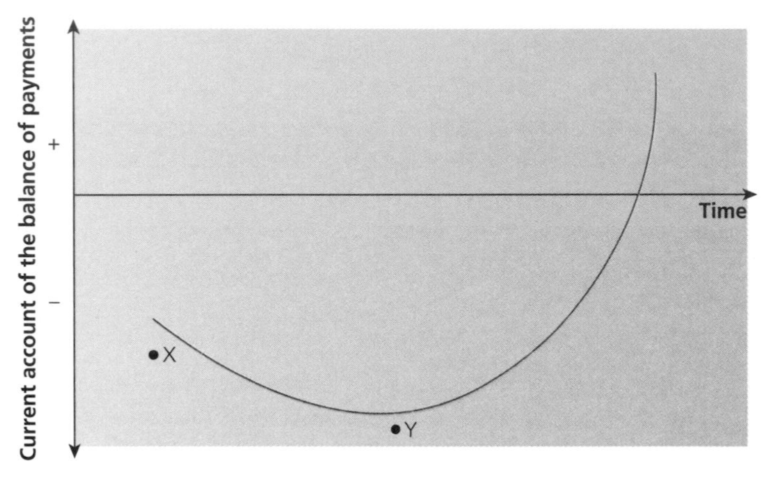

Figure 5.4 The J-curve effect

A further reason why depreciation might not lead to an improvement in the current account is because some firms might see depreciation as an opportunity to raise prices in order to increase profit margins.

Now test yourself

Tested

4 Which of the following is likely to cause an appreciation of the US dollar?
 (a) A rise in inward investment into the USA.
 (b) A rise in US inflation above that of its main competitors.
 (c) A rise in interest rates in other major economies.
 (d) An increase in confidence in the future state of the US economy.

5 Outline the likely effects of an appreciation of a currency on the country's economy.

Answers on p. 110

Monetary unions

These are trading blocs which have adopted a single currency.

Within the EU there is a European Monetary Union (EMU) in which the euro was launched in 1999 with 11 members. This increased to 17 by 2012 but the continuing crisis in the Eurozone has led to speculation that some members may leave or be forced to leave.

Benefits of membership of a monetary union

Revised

Many countries were keen to join EMU because they thought that it would enable them to gain advantages associated with greater integration with other countries with whom they conducted a significant amount of trade. These include:

- **Elimination of transaction costs:** these are costs involved in changing currencies when goods are imported or exported. Banks and financial institutions charge commission when exchanging currencies so the adoption of a single currency means that these no longer have to be paid. However, these costs are fairly insignificant because they are a very small proportion of GDP.
- **Price transparency:** a single currency means that consumers have the ability to compare prices more easily across national borders. This may reduce the likelihood of price discrimination although the geographical distances between countries and asymmetric information may not eliminate this practice.
- **Elimination of currency fluctuations between member countries:** with just one currency being used by member countries, businesses have increased certainty, which could encourage increased investment.
- **Increase in FDI:** it is argued that transnational companies might be encouraged to invest in countries which are part of a monetary union because they would save on transaction costs when they sell goods to other members of the union. However, there is little evidence that this impact is significant.

Costs of membership of a monetary union

Revised

- **Transition costs:** these are one-off costs associated with changing menus, price lists and slot machines when the currency is introduced. In practice, these are relatively insignificant.
- **Diversity of economies in the union:** it has become clear that, within the EMU, there is a great difference in the economies of the different countries. For example, labour costs in Greece, Italy and Portugal rose considerably relative to those in Germany during the period 2000–10. This makes economic management of the whole monetary union very problematic.
- **Loss of independent monetary policy:** countries no longer have control of their own interest rates. Instead they are set by the central bank of the union which, in the Eurozone's case, is the European Central Bank (ECB). The problem is that while some countries suffering from relatively high inflation rates require a higher interest rate, others with high unemployment and low inflation rates require a lower interest rate.
- **Loss of exchange rate flexibility:** individual members of the Eurozone use the euro and so no longer have their own currencies. This means that a country whose goods and service have become uncompetitive can no longer rely on a depreciation to restore competitiveness.
- **More stringent monetary policy:** in the case of the Eurozone, the ECB's inflation target is to keep inflation below 2%, which is more stringent than the UK's symmetrical target of 2% plus or minus 1%. This suggests that the ECB's target is more deflationary than the UK's.

International competitiveness

International competitiveness is a measure of a country's advantage or disadvantage in selling its products in international markets at a price and quality that is attractive in those markets. Two types of competitiveness may be distinguished:

- price competitiveness
- non-price competitiveness

Factors influencing international competitiveness

Revised

Price competitiveness may be affected by a variety of factors including the following:

- **Unit labour costs.** If unit labour costs are higher in one country than its competitors then its goods and services may be less competitive. To make international comparisons, the figures are converted into a single currency and expressed as an index number.
- **Productivity.** If labour productivity is higher in one country than its competitors then its goods and services are likely to be more competitive. Productivity is affected by a variety of factors including the amount and quality of capital per worker; the quality of human capital and the effectiveness of management. Comparisons may be made by comparing output per worker per hour worked.
- **The real exchange rate.** The **real exchange rate** is the **nominal exchange rate** adjusted for changes in price levels between countries. It may be calculated as follows:

  $$\text{real exchange rate} = \frac{\text{nominal exchange rate} \times \text{domestic price level}}{\text{foreign price level}}$$

  There will be a depreciation in the real exchange rate if the nominal exchange rate falls or if the prices of goods abroad rise relative to prices in this country. A fall in the exchange rate results in an increase in the competitiveness of a country's goods and services.

  On the other hand, there will be an appreciation in the real exchange rate if the nominal exchange rate rises or if the domestic price level rises relative to the foreign price level. A rise in the exchange rate results in a decrease in the competitiveness of a country's goods and services.
- **Labour taxes or subsidies.** Employers' national insurance contributions are regarded as a tax on jobs and so could reduce the competitiveness of a country's goods and services. In contrast, job subsidies might increase competitiveness. In the UK, the Employers Subsidy provides assistance for 6 months to firms taking on workers aged 18–24.
- **Government laws and regulations.** These include environmental and health and safety regulations; employment protection and anti-discriminatory laws; the national minimum wage and compulsory employer national insurance contributions.
- **Research and development (R&D).** A country which engages in a significant amount of R&D is more likely to attain greater technological advancement, so increasing its productivity.

The **real exchange rate** refers to how much the goods and services in the domestic country can be exchanged for the goods and services in a foreign country.

The **nominal exchange rate** is the rate at which one currency can be exchanged for another currency.

Now test yourself

Tested

6 How might each of the following affect the competitiveness of a country's goods and services?
(a) A depreciation in its exchange rate.
(b) A reduction in employer national insurance contributions.
(c) An increase in the national minimum wage.
(d) An increase in expenditure on research into new technology.
(e) An improved apprenticeship scheme for school-leavers.

Answers on p. 110

Measures of international competitiveness

Revised

International competitiveness is measured in a variety of ways, including some of those mentioned above:

- relative unit labour costs
- relative productivity measures

There are also some composite indices such as the **global competitive index**. This is based on a range of indicators including macroeconomic stability, labour market efficiency, infrastructure, health and primary education. According to this index the top ten most competitive economies in 2012 were:

1 Switzerland
2 Singapore
3 Finland
4 Sweden
5 Netherlands
6 Germany
7 United States
8 United Kingdom
9 Hong Kong SAR
10 Japan

The significance of international competitiveness

International competitiveness brings:

- an improvement in the current account of the balance of payments
- a reduction in unemployment
- an increase in economic growth because an increase in exports has a multiplier effect on national income

Polices to increase international competitiveness

Revised

Many of these policies are similar to those required to eliminate a balance of payments deficit on current account (see pages 56–7). For example:

- improved infrastructure
- training and education
- reduction in regulation and red tape
- modern apprenticeships
- reduction in employers' national insurance contributions

Also:

- **Tax incentives for firms to increase R&D:** these might result in the development of new technology which could lead to increases in productivity and lower average costs. Also, R&D might result in the development of new products and the improvement of existing products. Therefore R&D could help to improve both price competitiveness and non-price competitiveness.

- **Currency depreciation:** while currency depreciation would improve competitiveness it is important to note that it may be very difficult in practice for a country to engineer a change in the value of its currency under a system of floating exchange rates. A currency depreciation may be engineered by a cut in interest rates but in many countries this is in the hands of the central bank rather than the government. Alternatively, the central bank could sell its currency on the foreign exchange market. However, the amounts required may be considerable and difficult to sustain.
- **Protectionism:** again, this policy may not be realistic because it may be against the rules of the World Trade Organization (WTO) or against the rules of the trading bloc to which the country belongs.

Examiner's tip

A common response to a question about improving competitiveness is for the government to provide subsidies. However, these may also be outlawed by the WTO or the trading bloc to which the country belongs. Therefore, it is important to provide a context. For example, EU regulations do allow subsidises for the use of green technology so you could research examples to illustrate such exceptions.

Exam practice

Essay questions

1 **(a)** The USA fell from 5th to 7th place in the Global Competitiveness Index between 2011 and 2012. Examine the factors which might have caused a decrease in the international competitiveness of the USA's goods and services. [20]

(b) Evaluate strategies which may be used by businesses and governments to improve the competitiveness of a country's goods and services. [30]

2 Evaluate the benefits of membership of a monetary union such as the Eurozone. [30]

Data-response question

Extract 1: US trade disputes

For many years the Chinese currency, the renminbi, has been undervalued against the US dollar. This has made it very difficult for the USA to increase its exports, reduce its imports and create jobs.

The USA has also been involved in a variety of trade disputes which it has taken to the World Trade Organization (WTO). For example, the US government has alleged that China is using illegal subsidies which are causing unemployment and lower profits for US companies. Meanwhile, the USA has been accused by Brazil of imposing anti-dumping tariffs on its orange juice exports. The WTO found the action taken by the USA was illegal under its rules.

Brazil exports over $400 million-worth of orange juice to the USA. The WTO ruled that Brazil could impose tariffs on US goods amounting to $300 billion.

Further, Brazil persuaded the WTO that American government subsidies and loan guarantees to cotton growers violated WTO rules. This ruling allows Brazil to impose $560 million in retaliatory tariffs on cotton goods, beauty products and cars. This retaliation by Brazil could result in thousands of American workers losing their jobs.

Extract 2: The Chinese currency

The undervaluation of China's currency, the renminbi, against the dollar has been a source of tension between the USA and China for some time. The Chinese government kept the renminbi at 6.83 per dollar from mid-2008 until mid-2010 to protect its exporters from the global recession and a contraction in world trade. China has accumulated a record $2.4 trillion of reserves and $889 billion of US government debt, partly as a result of its exchange rate policy. It is suggested that global growth would be about 1.5% higher if China stopped undervaluing its currency and running trade surpluses.

The US trade deficit with China is not only due to the under-valuation of the renminbi but also because of a low savings ratio in the USA. An increase in Chinese spending and increasing savings in the USA would also help to reduce trade imbalances.

3 **(a)** With reference to the information provided and your own knowledge, explain the role of the World Trade Organization (WTO). [5]

(b) With reference to the information provided, analyse the effects of an undervaluation of the Chinese currency, the renminbi, for the US economy. [8]

(c) Apart from the undervaluation of the renminbi, examine two other factors which might explain the trade imbalance between the USA and China. [10]

(d) Assess whether trade imbalances are a problem for China. [12]

(e) With reference to Extract 1, assess the impact of tariffs, such as those imposed by the USA, on imported orange juice. Illustrate your answer with an appropriate diagram. [15]

Answers and quick quizzes online

Online

Examiner's summary

You should have an understanding of:

- ✔ The meaning of the balance of payments.
- ✔ The current account of the balance of payments.
- ✔ The financial account of the balance of payments.
- ✔ The causes of current account deficits and surpluses.
- ✔ The significance of current account imbalances.
- ✔ Measures to correct current account imbalances.
- ✔ Factors influencing the exchange rate of a currency.
- ✔ The significance of a depreciation of a currency.
- ✔ The benefits and costs of a monetary union.
- ✔ The meaning of international competitiveness.
- ✔ Factors influencing international competitiveness.
- ✔ Measures to improve international competitiveness.

6 Public finance, macroeconomic policies, and poverty and inequality

Public finance

There are three aspects to be considered:

- public expenditure
- taxation
- public-sector borrowing and public-sector debt

These are illustrated in Figure 6.1.

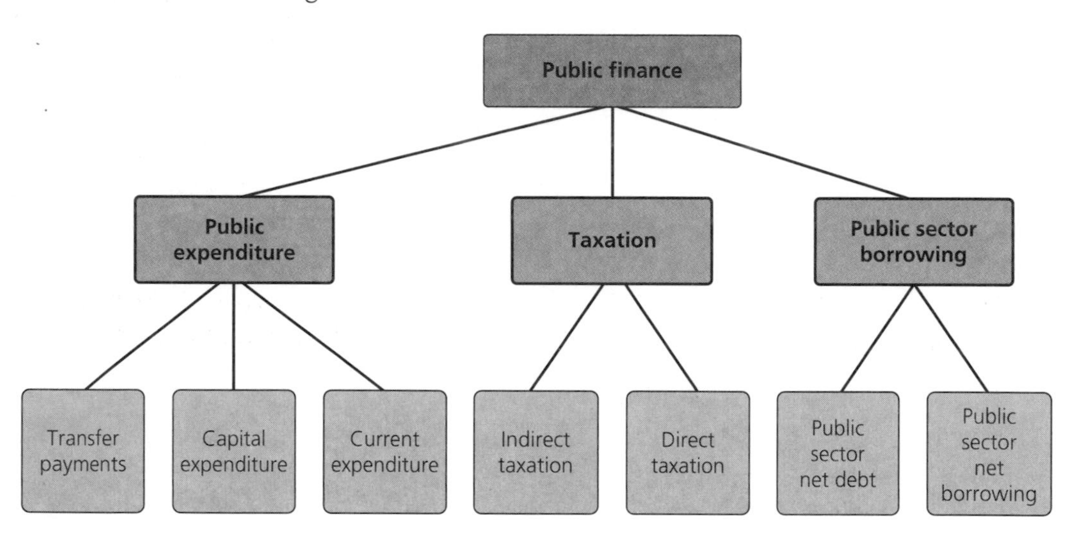

Figure 6.1 Key elements of public finance

Public expenditure

Revised

Public expenditure relates to expenditure by central government, local authorities and public-sector organisations. There are three broad elements of public expenditure:

- **Current expenditure:** this relates to the government's day-to-day expenditure on goods and services. Examples include:
  - wages and salaries of anyone employed directly by the state, e.g. civil servants, teachers and doctors
  - any consumable items such as drugs used by the NHS and energy used by the armed services
- **Capital expenditure:** this refers to long-term investment expenditure on capital projects such as Crossrail, new schools, new motorways and new tanks for the army.
- **Transfer payments:** these are payments made by the state to individuals without there being any exchange of goods or services. Typically, transfer payments are used as a means of redistributing income. UK examples include Employment and Support Allowance for ill and disabled people and the Job Seeker's Allowance for the unemployed.

Public expenditure is essentially money spent by the state or by a state-run organisation.

Typical mistake

Defining the term public expenditure as expenditure by the public — this is incorrect!

Examiner's tip

It is important to be able to distinguish between these three types of expenditure because their effects on the economy are very different.

Typical mistake

Confusion between the three types of public expenditure — in particular, it is important to remember that transfer payments are simply a means to redistribute incomes.

The objectives of public expenditure

Figure 6.2 provides a summary of the rationale for public expenditure.

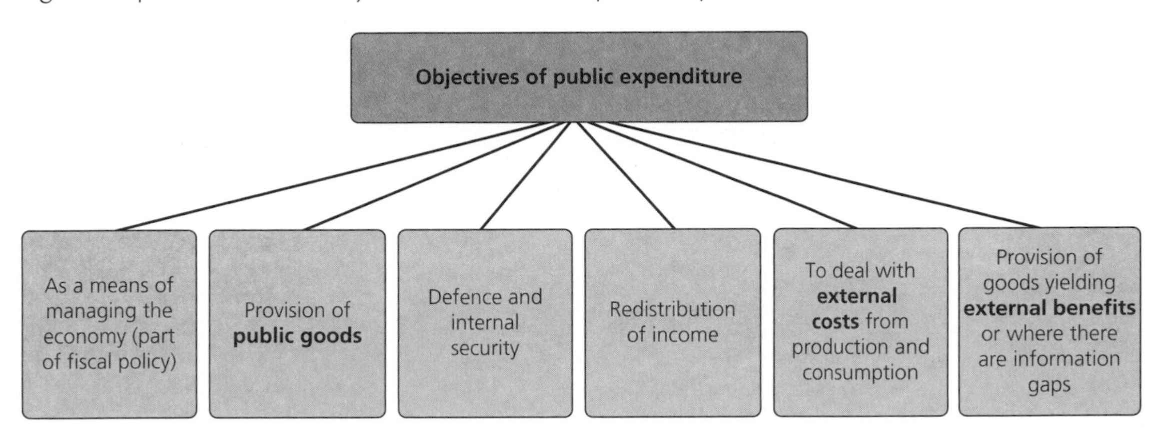

Figure 6.2 Objectives of public expenditure

The size of public expenditure

Several factors affect the size of public expenditure including:

- **The level of GDP:** in the long run, the amount that the government can spend depends on the amount that it can raise in taxation which, in turn, depends on the level of GDP. However, in the short run governments can borrow to finance an excess of public expenditure over tax revenues.
- **Demand for public services:** demand for many public services such as health and education is **income elastic**. Therefore, as incomes rise, the demand for these services rises more than proportionately.
- **Size and age distribution of the population:** as the size of the population rises, it invariably results in an increase in public expenditure. For example, there will be a greater demand for services provided by the state.

  An ageing population also places a greater burden on the state because the demand for medical services and social services increases while expenditure on benefit payments such as state pensions also rises.
- **The state of the economy:** when the economy is in recession, then public expenditure is likely to rise because of **automatic stabilisers** such as expenditure on Job Seeker's Allowance and housing benefits paid to people who have been made redundant.
- **Discretionary fiscal policy:** the 2008 financial crisis led to many governments providing a fiscal stimulus to their economies in the form of increased public expenditure and lower taxes. There is a sharp division of opinion among economists as to whether governments should be following **austerity measures** to reduce budget deficits or whether they should follow reflationary policies, e.g. increasing public expenditure, in order to stimulate economic growth.
- **Debt interest:** if the national debt has increased then in subsequent years the government will be paying larger and larger amounts in interest payments, so increasing public expenditure. In 2011–12, the UK paid nearly £50 billion in interest payments on its national debt but this is expected to increase to over £73 billion by 2014–15 because the government is running budget deficits, so adding to the national debt.

Public goods are goods which would be under-provided and under-consumed because they have two key characteristics: non-excludability and they are non-rivalrous.

External benefits are benefits to third parties who are not part of the transaction between a consumer and producer.

External costs are costs to third parties who are not part of the transaction between a consumer and producer.

Income elastic demand occurs when a change in real income causes a more than proportionate increase in demand.

Automatic stabilisers are changes in government spending or in tax revenue which occur automatically, without deliberate action by the government. (See also page 75.)

Austerity measures are measures taken to reduce government expenditure or expenditure by the country's citizens. The key aim is to reduce the budget deficit by bringing public expenditure more in line with tax revenues.

- **The rate of inflation:** in nominal terms public expenditure will inevitably increase during periods of inflation, not least because many benefits are **index-linked**, i.e. linked to the rate of inflation. Further, many public services are labour intensive and so wage costs tend to rise significantly if workers receive wage rises to compensate for the price rises.
- **Political factors:** governments might wish to improve public services or to redistribute income from the rich to the poor. This objective would almost inevitably lead to an increase in public expenditure.

Index-linked, in this context, implies that state benefits rise in line with the rate of inflation. In the UK, most benefits are now related to the Consumer Price Index (CPI) rather than the Retail Price Index (RPI).

The pattern of public expenditure

Figure 6.3 shows how public expenditure was distributed in 2012–13.

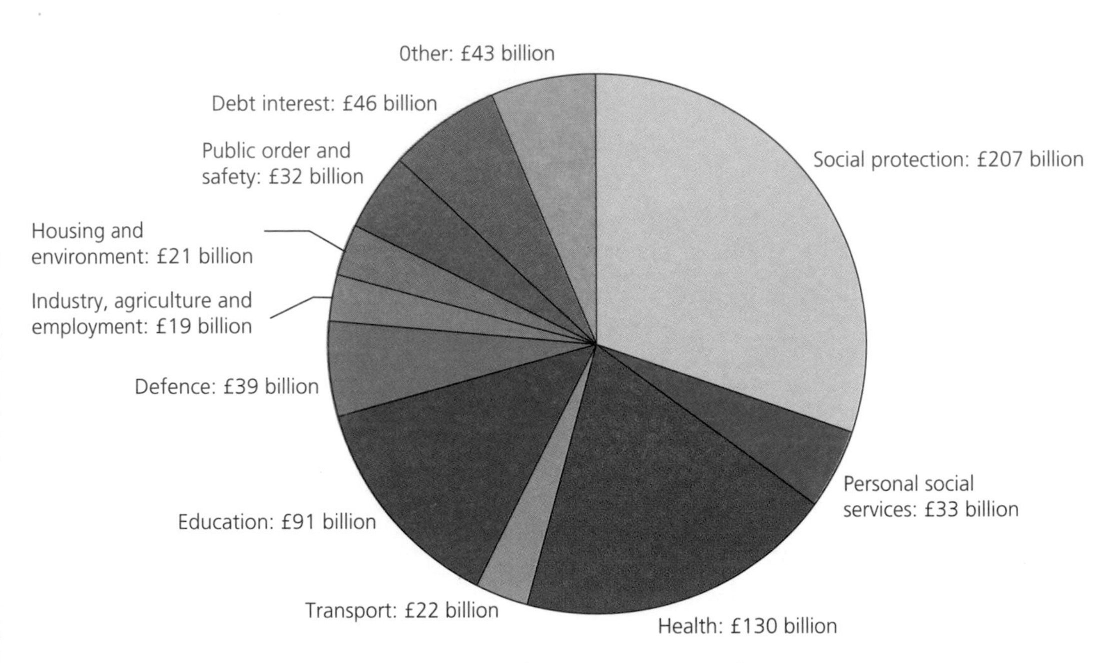

Figure 6.3 UK government expenditure 2012–13 (Source: HM Treasury)

This shows that the most significant areas of public expenditure are social protection (which includes the range of benefits), health and education. All three of these have increased as a share of total government expenditure in recent years partly because of:

- commitments made by the Labour Governments 1997–2010
- the ageing population
- increased benefits to pensioners and other groups

However, austerity measures are designed to limit or reduce benefits in the future. For example, the introduction of the Universal Credit in 2013, which has a maximum level, replaces a range of other benefits, such as:

- income-based Jobseeker's Allowance
- income-related Employment and Support Allowance
- Income Support
- Child Tax Credits
- Working Tax Credits
- Housing Benefit

Now test yourself

1. Why might expenditure on social benefits as a proportion of GDP be expected to increase in the future?
2. Which other areas of public expenditure might also be expected to increase as a proportion of GDP in the future? Explain your reasons.

Answers on p. 111

Tested

Taxation

Revised

This refers to the revenues received from taxpayers, which is used to finance public expenditure.

The objectives of taxation

Figure 6.4 summarises the main objectives of taxation.

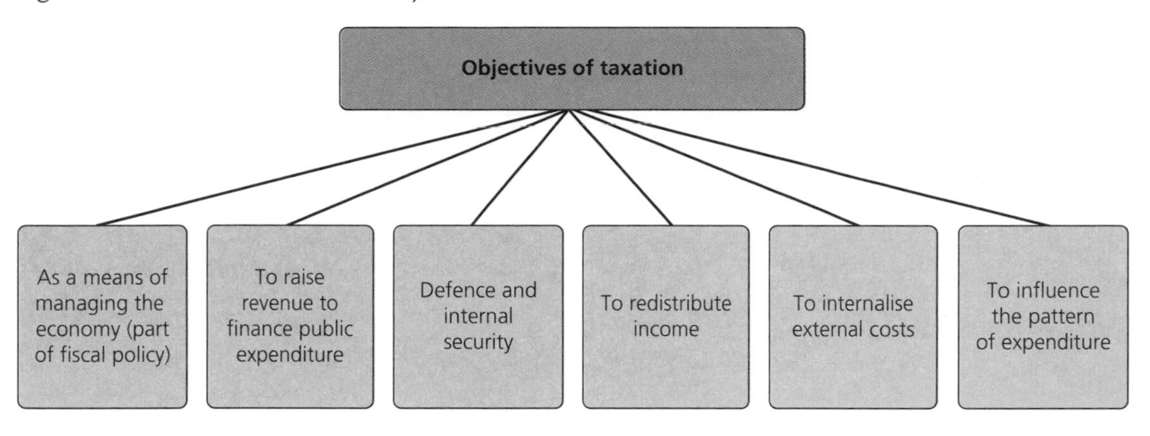

Figure 6.4 Objectives of taxation

Although some are similar to the objectives of public expenditure, there are some which are different. For example, taxes may be levied on producers and goods which cause external costs in an attempt to ensure that these costs are internalised.

Three categories of taxation

The effects of taxes on income distribution may be explained as follows:

- **Progressive tax:** is a tax in which the proportion of income paid in tax rises as income increases.
- **Proportional tax:** is a tax in which the proportion of income paid in tax remains constant as income increases.
- **Regressive tax:** is a tax in which the proportion of income paid in tax falls as income increases.

It is helpful to see how these taxes may be illustrated diagrammatically:

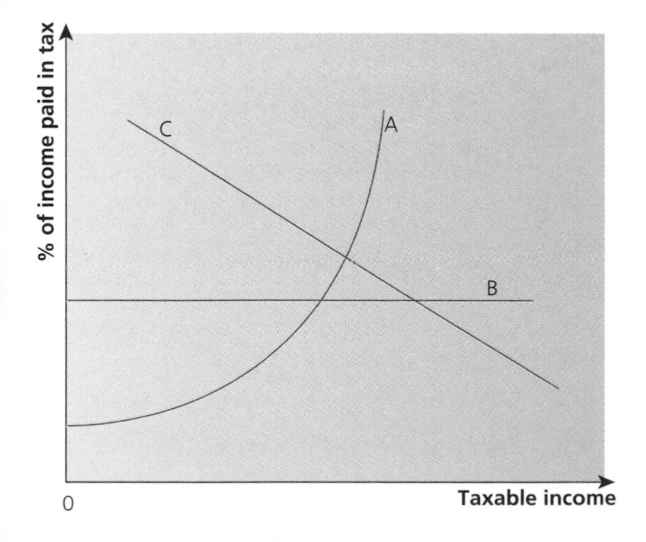

Figure 6.5 Categories of taxation

Tax A is a progressive tax; tax B is a proportional tax and tax C is a regressive tax.

Direct and indirect taxes

There are two broad groups of taxes: direct and indirect. **Direct taxes** are those levied on incomes and wealth and include:

- **Income tax:** a progressive tax levied at three rates: 20%; 40% and 45%.
- **Corporation tax:** a proportional tax on company profits, the rate of which will be reduced from 28% in 2010 to 21% in 2014. However, there is a lower rate of 20% for businesses making small profits.
- **Capital gains tax:** a tax on the increase in value of assets between the time they were bought and the time they were sold, e.g. on shares and investment property.
- **Inheritance tax:** a proportional tax on inherited assets levied at a rate of 40% on estates worth over £325,000.

Direct taxes are taxes on income and wealth.

Indirect taxes are taxes on expenditure.

Indirect taxes are taxes on expenditure and include:

- **Value added tax (VAT):** this is an *ad valorem* tax, i.e. a percentage of the price of the product.
- **Excise duties:** these are usually specific taxes, i.e. a set amount per unit.
- **Tariffs:** taxes on imported goods.

Examiner's tip

To determine whether a tax is direct or indirect consider whether it is levied directly on a person's income or on his/her expenditure.

Figure 6.6 shows the main sources of tax revenue for the UK.

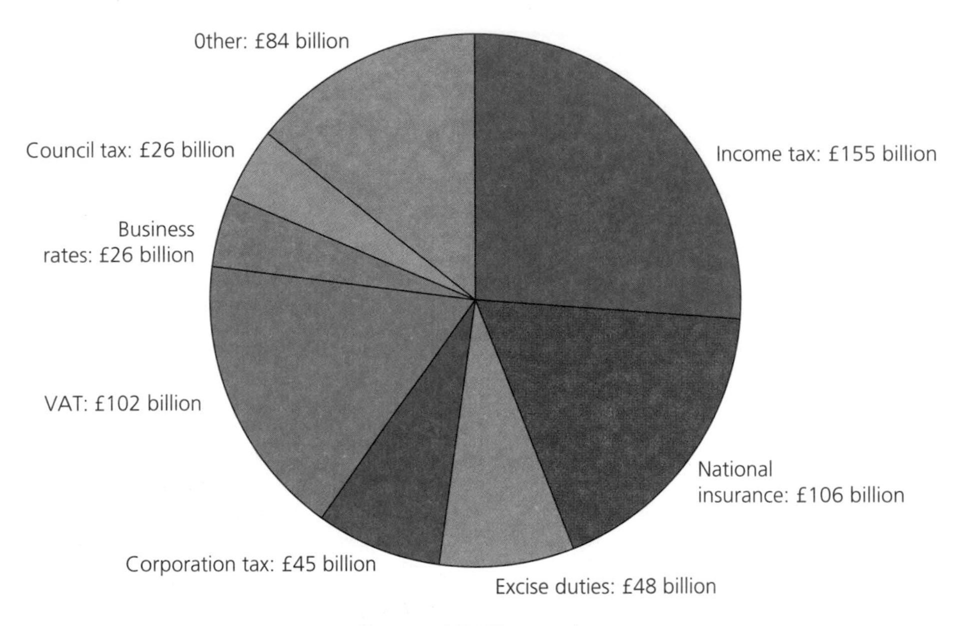

Figure 6.6 UK tax revenues 2012 (Source: HM Treasury)

Analysis of the effects of an increase in the rate of income tax

In the UK in 2010, an extra band of income tax of 50% was introduced but this was reduced to 45% in April 2013. In contrast, France has introduced two new tax rates on higher incomes and a new top rate tax of 75% on people earning incomes of over €1 million. The following illustrates the possible effects of such a rise in income tax:

- **On incentives to work:** an increase in income tax rates might cause a disincentive to work because:
  - the unemployed would be less willing to take jobs
  - those currently 'inactive' may be less willing to join the workforce
  - workers currently employed may be less willing to do overtime, more likely to reduce their working hours or retire early and less willing to apply for promotion

Typical mistake

It is often stated that VAT is a proportional tax because it is levied at a set rate. However, this is incorrect because VAT is a percentage of the price of a product and not based on income.

- **On tax revenues:** when the UK government introduced a new tax rate of 50%, it had been estimated that it would raise £2.5 billion but, in practice, it was calculated that it only raised £1 billion. Some argue that further increases in tax rates would cause tax revenues to fall. This may be explained using the **Laffer curve** shown in Figure 6.7

A **Laffer curve** is a chart showing the relationship between tax rates and tax revenues.

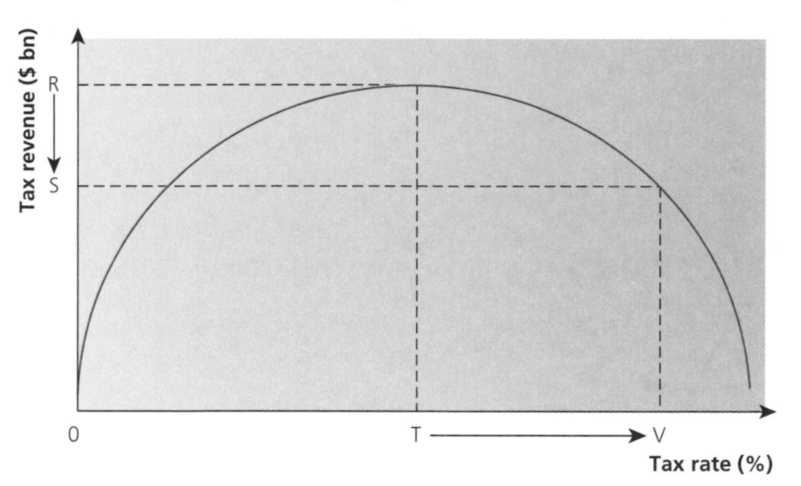

Figure 6.7 The Laffer curve

It can be seen that when the tax rate is increased up to point T, tax revenues increase. However, a further increase in the tax rate from T to V causes a fall in tax revenue from R to S. Several reasons might explain this phenomenon:
  - increased disincentives to work
  - an increase in tax avoidance, which is legal
  - an increase in tax evasion, which is illegal
  - a rise in the number of tax exiles (for example, it is expected that some high-income earners in France might move to the UK following the new tax rate of 75%)
- **On the rate of economic growth:** some economists argue that the disincentive effects described above might have an adverse impact on enterprise, so causing a fall in aggregate supply. Further, higher rates of income tax would cause a fall in disposable income, a fall in consumption and a fall in aggregate demand.
- **On the distribution of income:** an increase in income tax rates will make the tax system more progressive, so making income distribution more equitable.

Examiner's tip

Note that a change in direct tax rates can affect both aggregate demand (because it affects disposable income) and aggregate supply (because it affects incentives to work)

Now test yourself Tested

3 Why might an increase in income tax rates not result in an increase in government revenue?

Answers on p. 111

Analysis of the effects of an increase in the rate of VAT

- **On incentives to work:** an increase in the VAT rate might cause an incentive to work harder because workers will try to maintain living standards.
- **On tax revenues:** if the VAT rate increases, then tax revenues will almost certainly increase because VAT is applied to most goods and services. However, the tax revenue on goods and services whose demand is price elastic would fall.

- **On the rate of inflation:** a higher VAT rate would cause a one-off increase in prices. It would only be inflationary if trade unions and workers successfully bargained for higher wages which then resulted in a wage–price spiral.
- **On the rate of economic growth:** a higher rate of VAT would cause a fall in real income, which would cause a fall in consumption and a fall in aggregate demand so causing a reduction in the rate of economic growth. For businesses, the higher VAT rate would raise costs so causing a fall in aggregate supply, which would lead to a reduction in the rate of economic growth.
- **On the distribution of income:** research suggests that the impact of VAT is broadly regressive, so an increase in VAT would cause income distribution to become less even.

Now test yourself Tested

4 Why might higher excise duties on whisky not result in more tax revenue?

Answers on p. 111

Public sector net borrowing (PSNB) or fiscal (budget) deficit

Revised

The meaning of PSNB, fiscal deficit and budget deficit

These terms all imply that public expenditure is greater than tax revenues. A budget (fiscal) deficit may be cyclical or structural:

- The government's finances change in line with the trade cycle, i.e. they would usually be expected to deteriorate when the economy is in recession and to improve when economic growth is increasing.
- These are referred to as cyclical deficits and surpluses. A cyclical deficit is not regarded as a serious problem because it should disappear when the economy returns to its trend growth rate.
- However, a structural deficit remains even when the economy is operating at its full potential.

PSNB stands for public sector net borrowing and refers to a situation in which public expenditure is greater than tax revenue.

Examiner's tip

The terms PSNB, fiscal deficit and budget deficit are usually used synonymously although there are slight differences.

The significance of a structural budget deficit

This can only be assessed by examining the budget deficit as a proportion of GDP because this gives a better indication of the ability of the country to finance the deficit. However, if there is a persistent structural budget deficit, this might have serious implications for the economy. For example:

- **The national debt would increase:** successive years of budget deficit would cause an increase in the size of the national debt. This would result in increased interest payments on the national debt in the future, which may mean that there is less public expenditure available for public services, i.e. there will be an opportunity cost, perhaps in terms of new schools and hospitals.
- **Loss of AAA credit rating:** there may be a concern that the country might be unable to repay its debts in the future. If credit-ratings agencies reduce the country's credit rating, then it might have to pay a higher rate of interest on the bonds it sells to finance the national debt.

- **Crowding out:** structural deficits could imply that the size of the public sector is increasing. For example, in the UK, public expenditure increased from less than 37% of GDP in 1999 to over 46% of GDP in 2012. This could cause **resource or financial crowding out**.
- **Inflation:** if government expenditure is greater than tax revenues then injections are greater than withdrawals, so aggregate demand will increase which could cause inflationary pressure. Further, if the Bank of England directly funds the budget deficit, then the money supply would increase which, according to the Quantity Theory of Money, would result in inflation.
- **Decrease in FDI:** a persistent structural deficit may lead to a fall in FDI because of uncertainty concerning the future state of the economy.
- **Expenditure on infrastructure:** a structural deficit caused by significant investment on infrastructure and other capital goods may not be regarded as a serious problem because such expenditure would increase long-run aggregate supply and the growth prospects of the economy in the future.

Resource crowding out occurs when the economy is operating at full employment and the expansion of the public sector means that there is a shortage of resources in the private sector.

Financial crowding out occurs when the expansion of the state sector is financed by increased government borrowing. This causes an increased demand for loanable funds which drives up interest rates and crowds out private sector investment.

The meaning of national debt

This is the cumulative total of past government borrowing.

In 2012, the **national debt** exceeded £1 trillion but, as with the budget deficit, the absolute size is less significant than the national debt as a proportion of GDP. For many years until 2007, the national debt was below 40% of GDP but, following the financial crisis in 2008, it has risen rapidly and is expected to rise to over 76% by 2014–15.

National debt is the total sum owed by a government to holders of government bonds (called gilt-edged securities). In other words, it represents the total of a government's outstanding debt which it has accumulated over time.

The significance of the national debt

Many of the points made in relation to the significance of the budget deficit are relevant in this context. In particular, a large and increasing national debt could lead to:

- a loss of the country's AAA credit rating
- crowding out
- inflation
- decrease in FDI
- opportunity cost for future generations

In the long run, the government might be forced to raise taxes and/or reduce public expenditure so that budget surpluses can be used to reduce the national debt.

Typical mistake

Confusing the budget/fiscal deficit with the national debt.

Now test yourself

5 Explain the difference between the budget deficit and the national debt.
6 Suggest two reasons which might justify running a large budget deficit.
7 What might be the opportunity cost of an increasing national debt?

Answers on p. 111

Tested

Macroeconomic policies

Macroeconomic objectives

Revised

In a global context, different countries place a varying degree of emphasis on the following objectives.

1 Economic growth

For many developing and emerging countries, this is the key objective because it is seen as the means of reducing absolute poverty and increasing living standards. For developed countries, the promise of economic growth is often used by politicians as a means of securing election.

2 Sustainable growth

Sustainability is usually defined as the ability to meet the needs of the current generation without compromising the needs of future generations. Concerns have been expressed that rapid economic growth in countries such as China and India is unsustainable in terms of the environment and of natural resources. To the extent that climate change is man-made, it may be argued that the lifestyles of those in richer countries are unsustainable.

Sustainable growth is usually defined as growth that meets the needs of the present without compromising the ability of future generations to meet their own needs.

3 Full employment

This is usually defined as a situation in which the labour market is in equilibrium. However, this does not mean there is no unemployment. For example, there will always be some frictional unemployment. Given the rate of technological change and population growth, every economy needs to achieve a certain rate of economic growth to ensure that there is no increase in unemployment.

4 A low and stable rate of inflation

Inflation has serious disadvantages such as causing an arbitrary redistribution of income; uncertainty resulting in lower investment; and a reduction in real incomes. Further, if a country had a higher rate of inflation than its major trading nations, it would face a loss of competitiveness that could have adverse effects on its balance of payments on current account.

5 Balance of payments equilibrium on current account

As indicated previously (pages 57–8), global imbalances may be a source of global instability so countries may try to ensure that current account surpluses and deficits are kept to a minimum.

6 Redistribution of income

Most developed countries use a mixture of progressive taxes and means-tested benefits which are designed to redistribute income from the rich to the poor.

7 Fiscal balance

The financial crisis of 2008 began with a loss of confidence in the banking system. This has subsequently developed into a sovereign debt crisis with concerns that some countries will be unable to repay their debts. Therefore, fiscal balance may seem to be a desirable macroeconomic objective.

Examiner's tip

The above section and the one which follows on macroeconomic policies build on work covered in Unit 2, so it is important to recap your understanding of these areas. Remember that, in this unit, you may be required to apply these concepts in a global context.

Types of macroeconomic policies

Revised

There are two groups of macroeconomic policies:

- **Demand-side policies:** these policies are designed to influence aggregate demand and may be divided into fiscal policy and monetary policy.

- **Supply-side policies:** these are a range of policies which are aimed at increasing aggregate supply by increasing competitiveness, increasing incentives and increasing productivity.

In the context of Unit 4, these policies should be considered in a global context.

Fiscal policy

Revised

This relates to changes in government expenditure and taxation as a means of influencing the level of economic activity.

For a period after the Second World War until the 1970s, Keynesian demand-management techniques were followed by many countries. In this context, fiscal policy was used as a means of achieving a range of objectives including economic growth and full employment. However, governments became disillusioned with the use of fiscal policy to achieve these objectives because they appeared to be inherently inflationary.

In the aftermath of the 2008 financial crisis, many governments once again decided to employ fiscal policy measures as a means of stimulating their economies in order to prevent a depression.

There are two key features of fiscal policy: automatic stabilisers and discretionary fiscal policy.

Automatic stabilisers

Automatic stabilisers are changes in government expenditure and tax revenue which occur as GDP rises or falls without any change in government policy. In a recession, unemployment increases so the government spends more on unemployment benefits and other means-tested benefits. Such an increase in government expenditure is automatic.

In contrast, during a period of rapid economic growth the progressive tax system means that workers pay more tax as a proportion of their incomes and government expenditure on unemployment benefits falls.

Therefore, these stabilisers help to reduce fluctuations in the level of economic activity caused by the trade cycle.

Automatic stabilisers are changes in government expenditure and tax revenues which occur independently of any specific action by the government. They are determined by changes in the state of the economy.

Discretionary fiscal policy

Discretionary fiscal policy involves deliberate changes in public expenditure and taxation by the government in an attempt to influence the level of economic activity.

It is this type of policy that was used after the 2008 financial crisis.

The effectiveness of reflationary or expansionary fiscal policy depends on factors such as:

- The value of the multiplier.
- In the case of a cut in income tax rates, people may save their extra disposable income rather than spend it, or they may spend it on imports.
- The time lags involved.

Discretionary fiscal policy means deliberate changes in government expenditure and taxation in order to influence aggregate demand and, therefore, the level of economic activity.

- In the case of deflationary or contractionary fiscal policy, there may be significant disincentive effects when tax rates are increased. For example, if corporation tax is increased, this might cause a reduction in FDI while an increase in income tax rates might discourage unemployed workers from seeking work.

Monetary policy

Revised

This relates to changes in interest rates, money supply and exchange rates as a means of influencing the level of economic activity.

Control of inflation

As with fiscal policy, monetary policy has had a narrow role in many countries in the last 30 years, with the primary goal of controlling the rate of inflation.

Inflation targets have been used as a means to achieve this objective. The UK's target is 2% (although the Bank of England may allow the inflation rate to fluctuate between 1% and 3%) while that of the Eurozone countries is to keep inflation below 2%. This suggests that the Eurozone's target is more deflationary than the UK's.

New Zealand was the first country to officially adopt an inflation target in 1990 and many others have followed its lead including Chile, Canada, Brazil, Mexico and South Africa. In 2012, the US Federal Reserve also adopted a 2% inflation target.

Despite the apparent success of **inflation targeting** in keeping the rate of inflation relatively stable, critics argue that:

- The inflation target is too narrow and should be based on a wider range of variables, e.g. asset prices, commodity prices.
- Countries without inflation targets have also experienced relatively low rates of inflation.
- Following the slow rates of economic growth which occurred in the aftermath of the financial crisis, it might be desirable to have a higher inflation target.

Inflation targeting is a monetary policy strategy designed to maintain inflation at a certain rate or within a target range.

Quantitative easing (QE)

Quantitative easing is the process whereby the central bank buys government bonds and corporate bonds from commercial banks and other financial institutions so increasing liquidity in the banking system. This means that banks have more deposits and so will be in a better position to lend to private and business customers. By September 2012, the Bank of England had committed a total of £375 billion to QE, while the Federal Reserve had committed $1.4 trillion with a promise to spend a further $35 billion per month. Research into the effects of QE in the UK showed that:

- It had helped to increase the UK's annual economic output by between 1.5% and 2%.
- It caused an increase in the price of bonds and consequently a fall in their yield (market rate of interest).
- In turn, this is a major reason why deficits in company pension schemes have increased (because the yield on pension funds invested in bonds has fallen).

Quantitative easing is a process by which the Bank of England increases the money supply by buying government bonds and corporate bonds from financial institutions.

- Also, this fall in bond yields means that the annual income for a pensioner on an annuity has fallen.
- Consequently, it may be argued that there has been a redistribution of income away from pensioners.

Some economists argue that QE might be inflationary because it results in an increase in the money supply.

Now test yourself Tested

8 Outline two reasons why monetary policy might be ineffective as a means of stimulating economic activity.

Answers on p. 111

Supply-side policies

Revised

These refer to a range of policies aimed at improving the supply side of the economy by increasing competitiveness, increasing incentives and increasing productivity.

The more usual **labour-market policies** include:

- improvements in human capital through education and training
- reduction in trade union power
- reduction in unemployment benefits
- reduction in income tax rates
- reduction in employment protection legislation

Product-market policies include:

- privatisation
- promotion of new/small firms
- trade liberalisation

Capital-market policies include:

- reduction in corporation tax rates
- deregulation of financial markets

However, economists are becoming increasingly interested in new, modern supply-side policies. These include:

- **Nordic childcare schemes:** typically, these involve very large state subsidies towards pre-school nursery care. It has been estimated that, if such policies were followed in the UK, then about 1 million more women would be in the workforce.
- **Reduced incentives to remain unemployed:** in the UK, Employment and Support Allowance, which has replaced disability benefits, may only be claimed after a person has been assessed to determine his or her capability for work. Many of those who previously claimed benefits can no longer do so.
- **Focused immigration policies:** these would provide incentives for those of working age with skills in short supply to come to the country. Unfortunately, the UK's policy of setting a target for net migration is having serious adverse consequences for the supply side of the economy.

- **Local pay bargaining:** this would enable the labour market to operate more efficiently because in areas where, say, there was a shortage of nurses the wage rate would increase relative to areas where there was a surplus of nurses.
- **Modern apprenticeships:** these apprenticeships are work-based programmes that combine practical training with study and last for between 1 and 4 years.
- **Increased retirement age:** this increased the size of the labour force and allows those with substantial experience and skill to continue in productive employment.

Criticisms of supply-side policies

There are a number of criticisms of supply-side policies including:

- **Increased inequality:** income tax cuts and corporation tax cuts will often make the rich richer while measures such as cuts in unemployment benefits tend to make those already on low incomes poorer.
- **Exploitation:** a reduction in trade union power and in employment protection might result in the exploitation of workers.
- **Ineffectiveness:** if the economy is in recession and aggregate demand is already low then the policies may have little, or no, effect.
- **Market failure:** the deregulation of financial markets, for example, resulted in excessive risk-taking and the near-collapse of the banking system.
- **Time lags:** some supply-side measures would take a considerable time before having an effect. For example, measures to improve education are likely to take at least 5 years before they influence the productivity of the workforce.

Examiner's tip

Use supply-side policies which are relevant to the context of the country under consideration. For example, in the UK there are relatively few major industries which have not been privatised. However, the situation is rather different in countries such as Greece. As countries search for new ways to promote growth, it is likely that further supply-side policies will emerge.

Market failure means the failure of the market to allocate resources efficiently.

Now test yourself

Tested

9 What might be the fiscal implications of the following supply-side policies?
(a) A reduction in unemployment benefits.
(b) Higher subsidies for childcare.
(c) A reduction in corporation tax rates.

Answers on p. 111

Poverty

There are two broad measures of poverty: absolute poverty and relative poverty.

Absolute poverty

Revised

Usually, **absolute poverty** is defined as the minimum set of resources a person needs to survive including food, shelter, clothing, access to clean water, sanitation, education and information. It should be recognised that this definition is subjective because what 'a minimum set of resources' constitutes depends on value judgements. Further, as living standards and expectations increase, what constitutes a minimum level of income to meet basic needs will change over time.

Absolute poverty is when a person has insufficient resources to meet basic human needs, e.g. food, shelter, clothing.

Poverty is a multidimensional concept and other factors which may be used in assessing poverty include:

- the level of indebtedness
- the level of unemployment
- the extent of poor health or educational disadvantage
- the number of people living in inadequate housing and poor environmental conditions
- the extent to which people have inadequate access to public services
- the proportion of households having access to a given basket of goods and services

The measurement of absolute poverty

In 2008, the World Bank set the poverty line at $1.25 a day at 2005 GDP measured at **purchasing power parity**.

Relative poverty

Revised

Relative poverty is measured in comparison with other people in a country and will vary between countries. People are considered to be in relative poverty if they are living below a certain income threshold in a particular country.

People are considered to be in **relative poverty** if they are living below a certain income.

The measurement of relative poverty

A poverty line is set which is a percentage of average income. Commonly, these poverty lines range from 40–70% of average household income. In the EU people falling below 60% of median income are said to be 'at risk of poverty'. This gives an overall picture of the risk of poverty.

However, the figures can also be broken down by age, gender, household type and employment status to give a more detailed picture of who might be in relative poverty.

Typical mistake

Confusion between absolute and relative poverty.

Issues with the concept of relative poverty

- it is highly subjective
- it changes over time
- it cannot easily be used to make international comparisons

Now test yourself

10 If absolute poverty is falling, then will relative poverty be falling also?

Answers on p. 111

Tested

Other measures of poverty

Revised

- **The United Nations Human Poverty Index:** there are two indices, the first of which, HPI-1, is a measure of deprivation in the poorest countries of the world whereas HPI-2 is more relevant to developed countries. Both of these are composite measures which combine components such as life expectancy, literacy rates, long-term unemployment and relative income.
- **Standard basket of goods:** in this case poverty is calculated on the cost of a specific basket of goods and services that are regarded as being required for a basic standard of living.
- **Ratio method:** measured by calculating the proportion of income spent on basic necessities such as food or energy.

Inequality

Inequality can relate to both **income** and **wealth**.

Factors influencing inequality within a country

Revised

A variety of factors influence inequality in a country including:

- **Education, especially post-secondary education:** there is evidence suggesting that a person with a degree is likely to earn more than someone with two A-levels or equivalent, although much depends on the university, the subject and class of degree.
- **Training and skills:** similarly, skilled and highly trained workers typically earn significantly more than unskilled workers.
- **Wage rate:** this includes minimum wage rates.
- **Strength of trade unions**.
- **Degree of employment protection:** this factor, together with the strength of trade unions, has an impact on the wage rate and so influences income inequality.
- **Social benefits:** these provide a safety net for those on low incomes so if benefits are increased, especially means-tested benefits, then inequality is likely to decrease.
- **The tax system:** if the tax system is made more progressive, for example, then income inequality may be reduced.
- **Pensions:** pension entitlements can have a significant impact on inequality especially amongst the elderly.
- **Ownership of assets** (e.g. houses and shares): clearly, this factor has a major impact on the distribution of wealth.
- **Inheritance:** similarly, how much an individual or household inherits from relatives can have a significant effect on the distribution of wealth.

Typical mistake

Confusion between the terms 'income' and 'wealth'.

Income is a flow concept, for example, the money earned by a person over a period of time.

Wealth refers to the stock of assets a person owns.

Examiner's tip

It may be useful to distinguish between the factors contributing to income inequality and those contributing to wealth inequality.

Further causes of inequality within a country

Revised

Economic development

This is illustrated by the Kuznets curve as shown in Figure 6.8.

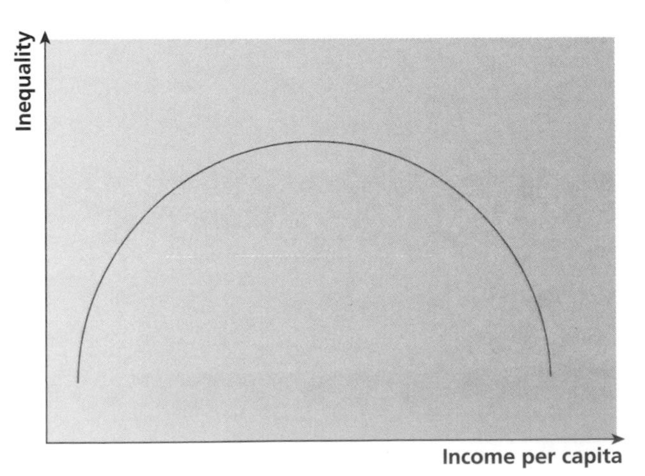

Figure 6.8 The Kuznets curve

This shows that when the economy is at an early stage of development and primarily agricultural, there is a relatively low level of income inequality. Industrialisation results in increased inequality but at some point it starts to decrease. This may be because governments have more resources to redistribute income. Kuznets provided evidence for his view when this theory was developed in 1955. However, in the 30 years before the financial crisis there was evidence that inequality in many advanced economies was increasing.

Globalisation

It is argued that globalisation has reduced inequality between countries. For example, industrialisation in China has resulted in a halving of people living in absolute poverty. However, there is some evidence that globalisation has increased inequality within countries. Reasons for this include:

- Unskilled workers in developed economies have faced a decline in their real wages or have been made redundant because wages in developing countries are often significantly lower.
- The market for highly skilled and talented workers is now global so such workers are able to command very high salaries.
- There has been a significant increase in the number of large TNCs and those at the top of these companies are often paid very high salaries.

Trade

Some economists argue that trade has increased inequality because large TNCs exert their monopsony power by driving down the prices they are prepared to pay for commodities from producers in developing and emerging economies.

Now test yourself

11 Identify two significant factors which influence inequality in the distribution of wealth.

Answers on p. 111

Tested

Measuring inequality

Revised

The Lorenz curve

Figure 6.9 illustrates a **Lorenz curve**.

Lorenz curve is a graphical representation of income distribution. For example, it might show that the poorest 10% of the population earns just 1% of the country's income.

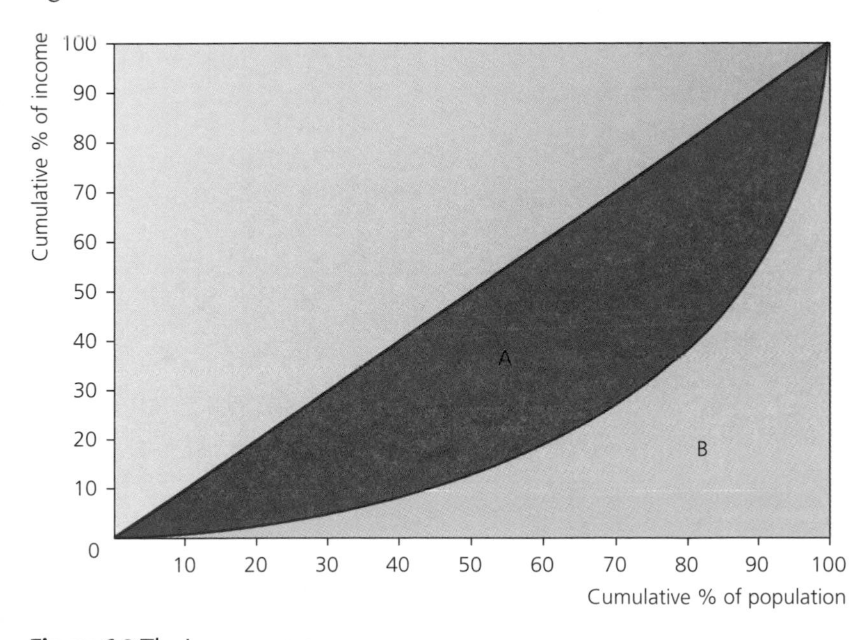

Figure 6.9 The Lorenz curve

It can be seen that the Lorenz curve plots the cumulative percentage of the population against the cumulative percentage of total income.

The 45° line represents perfect equality because the poorest 10% of the population receive 10% of the country's income; the poorest 20% of the population receive 20% of the country's income. The curved lined represents the income distribution for a particular country.

The Gini coefficient

To determine the degree of inequality, the **Gini coefficient** may be calculated. The following formula indicates how this may be done:

$$G = \frac{A}{A + B}$$

Where A represents the area between the diagonal line and the Lorenz curve and B represents the area under the Lorenz curve. The Gini coefficient will have a value between 0 and 1, with 0 representing absolute equality (the 45° line) and 1 representing absolute inequality (i.e. the Lorenz curve would lie along the horizontal and vertical axes).

The Gini coefficient may also be expressed as a percentage as shown below:

$$G = \frac{A}{A + B} \times 100$$

Now test yourself

12 How would an increase in inequality be illustrated on a Lorenz curve diagram?

Answers on p. 111

Tested

Typical mistake

Incorrect labelling of the Lorenz curve axes.

Gini coefficient: this is a numerical calculation of inequality based on the Lorenz curve with a value of zero being perfect equality and a value of 1 representing perfect inequality.

Significance and consequences of poverty and inequality

Revised

- Those in absolute poverty will have no collateral and so may be unable to secure a loan in order to start their own businesses.
- In countries where inequality is very high, there could be a significant number of people in absolute poverty.
- If there is a large proportion of the population living in absolute poverty, then the marginal propensity to save will be low. This will limit funds available for investment.
- In a country where there is great inequality, the rich may spend a large amount of their incomes on imported goods or they may transfer a large proportion of their incomes abroad (known as capital flight; see page 90).
- Inequality may result in a loss of social cohesion, which could have adverse consequences for growth. For example, the crime rate might increase and strikes might become more frequent.

Measures to reduce inequality

Revised

Given the potential problems which might be associated with inequality, most governments adopt policies to reduce the gap between the rich and the poor. These might include:

- Improved quality of education and training for the poor; in particular, governments might improve access to higher education for those from disadvantaged backgrounds.
- Making the tax system more progressive, for example by increasing the number of tax bands on incomes.
- Higher inheritance taxes: such a measure would have a significant impact on the distribution of wealth.

- Increasing the number and range of means-tested benefits so that transfer payments are targeted to those in greatest need.
- Measures to increase the geographical mobility of labour so that workers who are unemployed in one region can transfer to another region where employment is available.
- Introduction of or increase in the national minimum wage. This would help to prevent workers from being exploited

Exam practice

Essay questions

1 **(a)** Examine the causes of inequality in the UK or any country of your choice. [20]

(b) From April 2013, the UK's tax rates on income are 20%, 40% and 45%, the top rate having been reduced from 50%. Evaluate the likely economic effects of this tax change. [30]

2 **(a)** Many countries have experienced a substantial rise in their national debts since 2008. Assess the factors which might explain this trend in the public finances of a country of your choice. [20]

(b) Evaluate the case for cutting public expenditure rather than raising taxes as a means of reducing fiscal deficits. [30]

Data-response question

Extract: Public finances in the Eurozone

As part of conditions to bail out countries such as Greece, Ireland and Portugal the EU and the International Monetary Fund (IMF) imposed severe austerity measures which meant that the governments of these countries were forced to cut public expenditure and raise taxes. The effect of this has been to cause a fall in economic growth rates and rising unemployment in these countries.

Some economists such as Paul Krugman have suggested that a better strategy would be to adopt fiscal stimulus packages as a means of increasing growth and so improving public finances. However, other economists argue that governments should take immediate action to reduce their budget deficits and national debts because they are unsustainable and will be a huge burden on future generations.

Public finances, growth rates and unemployment rates in selected Eurozone countries in 2011 are shown in the table.

Country	Budget deficit % of GDP	National debt % of GDP	Growth rate %	Unemployment rate %
Germany	0.8	81.8	2.7	6.0
Greece	9.4	161.7	−6.0	17.3
Ireland	13.4	105.4	0.7	14.4
Portugal	4.4	112.8	−2.2	12.7
Spain	9.4	68.1	0.7	21.7

3 **(a)** Explain the effect of an increase in a country's budget deficit on its national debt. Refer to a country of your choice in your answer. [5]

(b) Analyse the implications of a recession on the UK's public finances. [8]

(c) Assess the factors which might explain why the growth rate of some Eurozone countries is expected to be lower than that of Germany. [10]

(d) Examine policies which might be used by countries such as Ireland and Spain to make their goods and services more competitive. [12]

(e) Evaluate the case for Eurozone countries which are in recession to adopt stimulus packages. [15]

Answers and quick quizzes online

Online

Examiner's summary

You should have an understanding of:

- ✔ Public expenditure: current, capital and transfer payments.
- ✔ Taxation: progressive, proportional and regressive taxes; direct and indirect taxation.
- ✔ Public-sector borrowing: budget deficits and national debts.
- ✔ Key macroeconomic objectives.
- ✔ Macroeconomic policies: fiscal, monetary and supply-side policies.
- ✔ Poverty, absolute and relative.
- ✔ Causes of inequality.
- ✔ Measures of inequality: Lorenz curves and Gini coefficients.
- ✔ Measures to reduce inequality.

7 Growth and development

Economic development

Distinction between growth and development

Revised

- **Economic growth:** this refers to the growth in the productive capacity of the economy and would be represented by an outward movement of the productive possibility frontier or a rightward shift in the long-run aggregate supply curve. It is usually measured by referring to changes in real GDP. Therefore, economic growth is a positive economic concept.
- **Economic development:** this refers to an improvement in living standards and welfare over time. Clearly, what constitutes development is subjective, depending on a person's value judgements. Therefore, economic development is a normative economic concept.

Economic growth means increase in real GDP.

Economic development involves an improvement in economic welfare, measured in a variety of ways.

Measuring economic development

Revised

Given the subjective nature of economic development, there is no single measure which could capture its essence. However, there is a composite measure which is used in the United Nations Development Report called the Human Development Index (HDI). This consists of three elements:

- GDP per head — measured at purchasing power parity.
- Health — measured in terms of life expectancy at birth.
- Education — measured in terms of mean years of schooling at age 25 and expected years of schooling at age 4.

However, this measure is fairly narrow and ignores a range of other indicators which may be regarded as significant for development. These include:

- the proportion of the population with access to clean water
- the proportion of the male population employed in agriculture
- energy consumption per person
- the proportion of the population with internet access
- mobile phones per thousand of population

Some economists would go further and suggest that factors such as civil rights and the degree of democracy and inequality are important indicators of development.

Examiner's tip

When discussing economic development, it is useful to know a range of development indicators.

Typical mistake

Inability to distinguish between economic growth and economic development.

Limits to economic growth and development

The following factors relate primarily to developing economies but several factors will also apply to advanced economies.

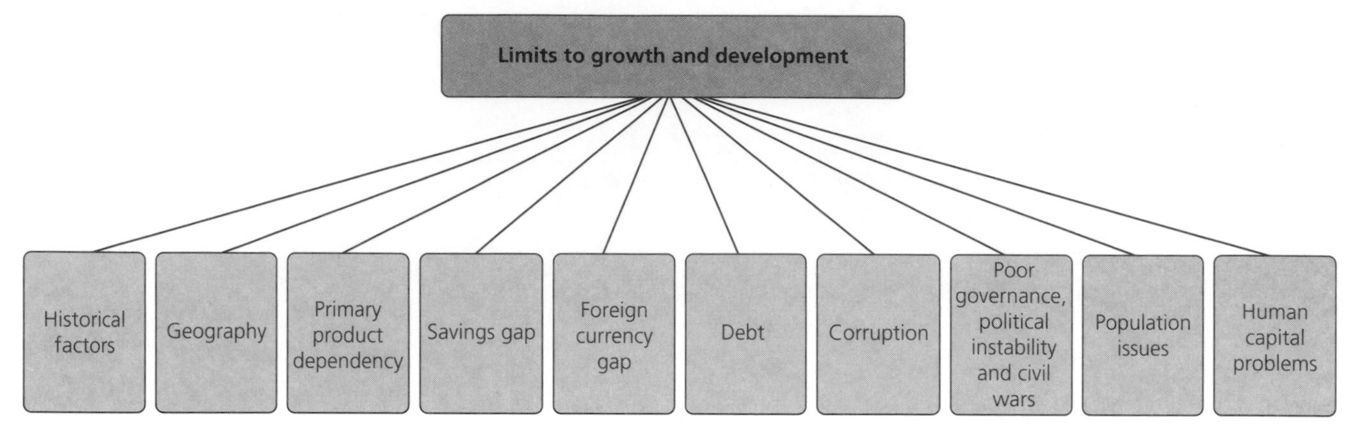

Figure 7.1 Limits to growth and development

Figure 7.1 illustrates some factors which hinder a country's growth and development. This is not an exhaustive list: when examining a particular country other factors may be of greater significance. It is important, therefore, to undertake some case studies of individual countries to gain a deeper understanding of the issues which have prevented growth and development.

Examiner's tip

The factors identified above are not an exhaustive list and are best understood by reference to case studies of particular countries.

Geographical and historical factors

Revised

Geography

Some countries face particular problems because they are land-locked (having no access to the sea). This may act as a constraint on development because the country may have no direct access to markets abroad, especially if the road infrastructure is poor. Further, if a country is not geographically close to a large market then this might hinder progress because producers might not be able to sell products easily.

History

There is considerable debate about the impact of colonialism on growth and development in former colonies. Some suggest that colonialism encouraged the culture of dependency and led to the exploitation of resources by rich countries. These factors left a poor legacy and contributed to weak growth and development when the colonies became independent. On the other hand, others argue that colonialism contributed to growth and development because the ruling country invested in infrastructure and education. The impact of colonialism was different in different countries as evidenced by the very different paths of Malaysia and Ghana following independence.

Examiner's tip

To enhance your understanding, prepare case studies for at least one country from each of the following continents: Asia, Africa and South America.

Primary product dependency

Revised

There are two broad types of primary product:

- **Hard commodities** are usually those that are mined or extracted, e.g. copper, tin, silver, platinum, lithium and iron ore.
- **Soft commodities** are usually agricultural goods, e.g. wheat, rice, palm oil, citrus fruits and barley.

Primary product dependency occurs where production of primary products accounts for a large proportion of a country's GDP.

Examples of countries that have a high dependency on primary products are given below:

Chile	Copper, fruit and frozen juices
Peru	Fish products, minerals (gold, silver, copper, zinc, lead), agricultural products (coffee, asparagus)
Ghana	Gold, oil and cocoa
Kenya	Tea, horticulture
Nigeria	Oil

Disadvantages of primary product dependency

For countries dependent on primary products, there are various problems:

- **Extreme price fluctuations:** both the price elasticity of demand and the price elasticity of supply for primary products tend to be inelastic. Consequently, any demand-side or supply-side shock will cause a large price change.
- **Fluctuations in producers' revenues:** the price fluctuations described above will cause fluctuations in producers' incomes since demand is price inelastic. Therefore, a fall in price would cause a fall in total revenue while a rise in price would cause an increase in total revenue of producers. These price and revenue fluctuations make it more difficult to plan investment and output.
- **Fluctuations in foreign exchange earnings:** revenues from exports of primary products will also fluctuate in the same way as those for primary product producers. This may make it more difficult for the government to plan economic development.
- **Protectionism by developed countries:** many developed countries use protectionist measures to prevent developing countries having free access to their markets, making it more difficult for poorer countries to grow and develop.
- **Shortages of supplies for domestic consumption:** cash crops are usually exported, meaning that there is little left for domestic consumption.
- **Finite supplies of hard commodities:** eventually, supplies of commodities such as copper or gold will be exhausted so it is important that there has been some diversification into other industries before that happens.
- **Appreciation of the currency:** demand for a particular commodity will cause an increase in demand for the country's currency resulting in an appreciation of the currency. This will reduce the competitiveness of the country's manufactured exports.
- **Falling terms of trade:** the Prebisch–Singer hypothesis (see next page).

Now test yourself Tested

1 Using a diagram, explain why prices of primary products are likely to fluctuate.

Answers on p. 111

The Prebisch–Singer hypothesis

The key elements of this theory are:

- Demand for primary products tends to be income inelastic whereas the demand for manufactured goods is income elastic.
- Therefore, as real incomes rise, the demand for manufactured goods will increase at a faster rate than the demand for primary products.
- As a result, the prices of manufactured goods will rise more quickly than the prices of primary products.
- Consequently, the terms of trade of developing countries will fall relative to those of developed countries.

As explained in Chapter 4, the terms of trade (T/T) refer to the price of exports relative to the price of imports, or how much must be exported to gain a certain quantity of imports. (See page 44 for the method of calculating terms of trade.)

This implies that the developing country will have to export more to gain a given quantity of imports.

Falling terms of trade have often contributed to a deterioration in the current account of the balance of payments of developing countries. In turn, this has led to these countries running up large external debts.

Typical mistake

Confusion between the terms of trade and the balance of trade. To avoid this confusion remember that the terms of trade relate to relative prices of exports and imports whereas the balance of trade relates to the value (i.e. price × volume) of exports and imports.

Criticisms of the Prebisch–Singer hypothesis

- Some countries have developed on the basis of primary products, for example Botswana: diamonds; and Chile: copper. Further, countries such as Bolivia have nearly half the world's known reserves of lithium — used to make batteries for hybrid and electric cars. Given the subsidies being given to companies to develop electric cars and the decline in oil production, demand for lithium can be expected to rise rapidly in the future.
- If a developing country, such as Kenya, has a comparative advantage in tea, then its resources will be used more efficiently by specialising in the production of tea.
- During the years 2000–08, primary product prices rose sharply while the prices of many manufactured goods were falling. This caused the terms of trade of developing countries to increase.
- There is a belief that, with rising real incomes and populations in sub-Saharan African countries, India and China, food and commodity prices are expected to continue on an upward path.
- FDI has increased significantly in recent years in countries dependent on primary products. This has helped them to grow and develop.

Examiner's tip

Remember to apply synoptic concepts when discussing primary product dependency, for example, price elasticity of demand, total revenue, balance of payments and income elasticity of demand.

Now test yourself Tested

2 **(a)** Calculate the change in the terms of trade from the following information: import prices rise by 4% while export prices rise by 12%.

(b) Outline two implications of this change in the terms of trade.

Answers on p. 111

Savings gap

Revised

The Harrod–Domar model illustrates the problem of how countries with a low GDP per head will experience low **savings ratios** (because their **marginal propensity to consume** will be high). Low savings mean that it will be difficult to finance investment and, with low levels of investment, **capital accumulation** will be limited. This will translate into low output and GDP as illustrated in Figure 7.2.

Savings ratio: savings as a proportion of GDP.

Marginal propensity to consume: the proportion of any increase in income which is spent.

Capital accumulation: additions to the capital stock of a country which may then be used to produce other goods and services.

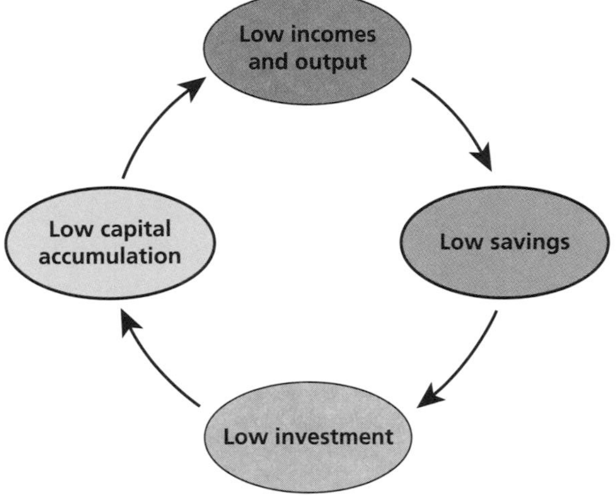

Figure 7.2 The Harrod–Domar model

However, this model may be criticised because:

- it focuses on physical capital and ignores the significance of human capital
- it assumes a constant relationship between capital and output
- the savings gap may be filled by means other than domestic savings (see pages 101–3)

Now test yourself Tested

3 What is the main cause of the savings gap in developing countries?

Answers on p. 112

Foreign currency gap

Revised

Countries may face shortages of foreign currency, which could be caused by:

- dependency on the export of primary products
- dependency on imports of oil and manufactured goods

- interest payments on debt to foreign countries
- **capital flight**, which occurs when individuals and countries decide to transfer cash deposits to foreign banks or to buy shares or assets in foreign countries. Inevitably, capital flight would contribute to both the savings gap and foreign exchange gaps and consequently restrict economic growth. Further, it reduces the country's tax base because any potential tax payable on those assets will be lost.

Capital flight occurs when assets or money are taken out of a country.

These factors could limit development because the country would have insufficient foreign currency to purchase imported capital goods which might be needed to increase productive capacity.

Now test yourself

Tested

4 How might the foreign exchange gap constrain economic development?

Answers on p. 112

Debt

Revised

The causes of the increase in the external debts of many developing countries lie in a variety of factors:

- Dependency of primary products and falling terms of trade (see above).
- Developing countries may have borrowed money at times of low interest rates, only to find that they struggled to service the debt (i.e. pay interest on it) some years later when interest rates increased.
- When oil prices increased, these countries had to borrow to pay for imports.
- Decisions to borrow money to finance prestigious investment projects at times when the world economy was growing strongly and/or when the prices of the goods they were exporting were high.
- Depreciation in the value of the currencies of developing countries which increased the burden of the debt.
- Loans taken to finance expenditure on military equipment.

Corruption

Revised

This is the use of power for personal gain and it may take various forms including bribery, extortion and diversion of resources to the governing elite. Corruption can cause:

- an inefficient allocation of resources
- an increase in costs of doing business in the country
- a decrease in foreign direct investment
- capital flight

All of the above would result in a slower rate of economic growth and economic development.

Poor governance, political instability and civil wars

Revised

If there is weak or inefficient government then it is unlikely that resources will be allocated efficiently. Further, **government failure** may occur, i.e. intervention by the government in the economy might result in a net welfare loss.

Civil wars can have a devastating effect on the infrastructure of the country which can hinder growth and development. Further, there may be a substantial loss of life which could reduce the size of the working population and reduce the country's productive potential. Once again, civil wars would deter both domestic investment and foreign direct investment.

Government failure occurs when intervention by a government causes a movement further away from the socially optimum level of output.

Population issues

Revised

- After growing slowly for most of human history, the world's population more than doubled in the last half of the twentieth century to 6 billion in 1999. Lower mortality rates, longer life expectancy and large youth populations in countries where fertility remains high have all contributed to the rapid population growth. By 2050, the population is expected to be over 9 billion.
- Virtually all of this population growth is expected to be in developing countries and will be mainly among the poorest populations in urban areas. In particular, the population of sub-Saharan Africa is projected to triple from 1.2 billion to 4.2 billion during the twenty-first century. Countries such as Malawi and Mozambique are likely to experience particularly rapid population growth rates.
- Meanwhile, the population of intermediate-fertility countries, such as the United States, Mexico and India, will increase by just 26%, while that of low-fertility countries, which includes most of Europe, China and Australia, will decline by about 20%.
- Population growth may be analysed by reference to the views of Thomas Malthus. He predicted that famine was inevitable because population grows in geometric progression whereas food production grows in arithmetic progression. Although his predictions proved incorrect for Britain in the nineteenth century, some economists believe that they are still relevant for some of the poorest countries in sub-Saharan Africa, as described above.
- In countries where population growth is greater than the growth of GDP, then GDP per head would decline.
- Apart from the growth in size of population, there is also the issue of ageing populations. This may have some significant implications. For example, smaller working populations will have to support much larger proportions of elderly people. This will be an issue not only for countries in Western Europe but also for China and Japan.

Now test yourself Tested

5 Under what circumstances would an increase in economic growth be associated with a fall in GDP per head?

Answers on p. 112

Human capital inadequacies

Revised

If the school enrolment ratio is low then the levels of literacy and numeracy are likely to be low. In turn, it is likely that:

- the productivity of the workforce is likely to be low
- this will act as a deterrent to FDI

HIV/AIDs

A further problem is that if an adult develops AIDs, he or she may be forced to give up work. The adult's children might be withdrawn from school either because the school fees can no longer be afforded or because children are required to work at home. If teachers also contract AIDs then they may be forced to give up work. Overall, the quality of education is likely to deteriorate.

Policies to promote growth and development

A variety of strategies have been used to promote growth and development in different countries. What may appear to be very successful in one country might be completely inappropriate and/or ineffective in another country. Factors such as the country's history, natural resources, geography and culture, and the skills and enterprise of the workforce may have a significant impact on the success of the strategies employed. In practice, a combination of strategies is likely to be more effective than reliance on one approach only.

Figure 7.3 indicates a number of different policies which might be adopted to promote growth and development.

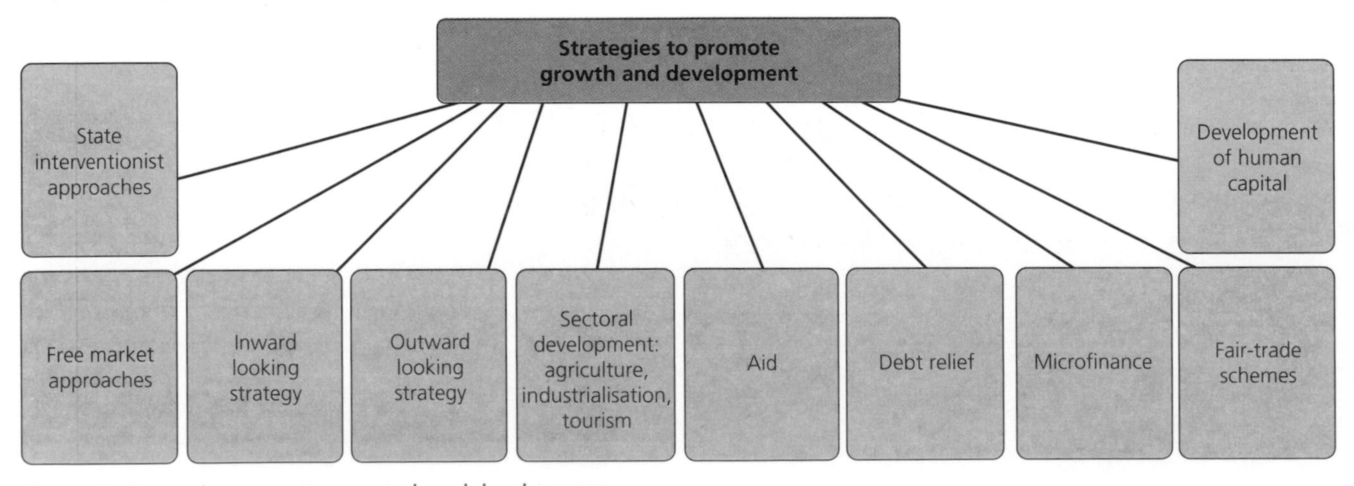

Figure 7.3 Strategies to promote growth and development

State interventionist approach

Revised

For a significant period following the Second World War interventionist policies were followed by many developing countries on the basis that the free market would be unable to provide a suitable basis for economic development.

State intervention took many forms including:

- **Import substitution:** industrialisation was seen as key to economic development. Therefore, countries protected domestic firms so that foreign imports could be replaced by domestic production.
- **Nationalisation:** this refers to the transfer of ownership from the private sector to state control of key industries such as energy, transport and certain manufacturing companies of strategic importance.
- **Price subsidies:** the government subsidised certain goods regarded as necessities such as basic foods.
- **Over-valued exchange rates:** governments often tried to maintain the exchange rate at an artificially high level in order to keep down the cost of imported raw materials and finished goods.
- **State-controlled boards:** these boards were set up by governments in many developing countries. They forced farmers to sell their produce to these boards at low prices so that the goods could be sold to consumers cheaply.

Import substitution refers to policies designed to replace imports with domestically produced goods.

Nationalisation occurs when privately owned firms and industries are brought under state control.

By the end of the 1970s, there was increasing disillusion with such interventionist policies because they were associated with various problems including:

- Low rates of economic growth — a large state sector tended to stifle competition and enterprise which translated into low productivity rates so resulting in slow growth.
- Resource and allocative inefficiency — the absence of the profit motive and only limited competition meant that firms did not produce at the output at which price is equal to marginal cost.
- Government failure — this occurs when intervention by the government causes a movement further away from the socially optimal output.
- Corruption — with a large state sector and increased government intervention, there was a large increase in the number of civil servants in many developing countries, which provided more scope for corruption.
- Increasing fiscal deficits — these arose because of food subsidies and losses arising from inefficient nationalised industries.
- Increasing balance of payments deficits on current account — these were associated with over-valued exchange rates.

Examiner's tip

Many of the terms included in this section have appeared in previous units, and a precise understanding of those concepts is essential.

Free-market approaches

Revised

A shift in the political landscape in the 1980s with the election of Margaret Thatcher in the UK and Ronald Reagan in the USA, both following right-wing political agendas, resulted in a move towards free-market approaches and outward-looking strategies as the best ways of promoting growth and development.

The basis for this approach was found in two key principles:

- **Free-market analysis**, which assumes markets operate efficiently and consumers and producers act rationally. The free market is, therefore, the best way to allocate resources.
- **Public choice theory**, which is based on the assumption that politicians, civil servants and governments use their power for their own self-interest.

Implementing a strategy based on free-market approaches would involve:

- **Trade liberalisation:** this implies the removal of protectionist barriers so making it easier to trade. In turn, this is likely to encourage FDI.
- **Market liberalisation:** this relates to a range of policies, for example that nationalised industries are privatised and that there is an emphasis on deregulation and measures to promote competition between firms.
- **Supply-side policies:** (see section on pages 77–8).
- **Structural adjustment policies:** these are designed to eliminate budget deficits and current account deficits. They include the policies identified above as well as:
  - abolishing food and agricultural subsidies to reduce government expenditures
  - deep cuts to social programmes such as health, education and housing
  - devaluation of the currency to increase the competitiveness of the country's goods

Trade liberalisation refers to measures designed to promote trade by the removal of protectionist barriers, such as tariffs and quotas.

These policies had a very harsh impact on some developing countries, especially on their poor, because of the removal of food subsidies and cuts to social programmes. Consequently, there has been some modification to this approach since the start of the century. In particular, there has been a recognition that there are imperfections in the product and labour market which mean that the free market does not necessarily allocate resources efficiently. These imperfections include:

- **Asymmetric information** — for example, consumers may have much less information than producers so may not be able to make rational choices.
- **Externalities** — these are costs and benefits which affect third parties not directly involved in the transaction. Therefore, they would not be reflected in the market price.
- **Absence of property rights** — Hernando de Soto has argued that a strong market economy depends critically on property (ownership) rights and the rule of law. For example, if a person owns no assets then it will be very difficult for him/her to secure a bank loan because they do not have collateral. Further, without a legal system the market will fail.
- **Monopolies** — consumers may face only a single supplier of a product or service. This means there is no choice and price may be greater than marginal cost so there is allocative inefficiency.

Asymmetric information occurs when some agents in the market, e.g. producers, have more information than other agents, e.g. consumers.

Property rights are ownership rights based on a legal structure.

Examiner's tip

Much of the above section is based on work covered in Unit 1 so revision of the key elements of that unit would be helpful.

Inward-looking and outward-looking strategies

Revised

Inward-looking and **outward-looking strategies** may appear to be complete opposites. In practice, a number of developing countries have used these at different stages of their development. At an early stage of development, countries may be more inclined to adopt inward-looking strategies. These enable a country to develop its manufacturing industry under the cover of protectionism. Then, when companies have gained economies of scale and are strong enough to withstand foreign competition, the countries may adopt more outward-looking strategies.

Inward-looking strategies refer to industrialisation based on import substitution, i.e. the country tries to industrialise by replacing imported manufactured goods with domestically produced goods.

Outward-looking strategies refer to a set of policies based on a free-market approach, e.g. removal of trade barriers and a reduction in state intervention in the economy.

Inward-looking strategies

These are often associated with interventionist strategies (see above) and they are characterised by:

- **Import substitution**, which occurs when imports are replaced by goods produced in the domestic economy.
- **Protectionism**, under which policies would include tariffs, quotas and, in particular, subsidies to domestic producers.
- **Restrictions on FDI**.

It can be seen that such policies are inward looking in the sense that they are focused on developing domestic firms. However, there are certain problems associated with inward-looking strategies including:

- Distortion of comparative advantage — protectionism would result in a misallocation of resources.
- Restriction of competition — which could result in inefficiency.

Outward-looking strategies

As the term suggests, this approach is outward looking with a focus on greater integration with the global economy. These strategies are characterised by:

- **Trade liberalisation** (i.e. removal of trade barriers): this results in an increase in trade which brings welfare benefits, for example in terms of lower prices and increased consumers' surplus. This is illustrated in Figure 7.4.

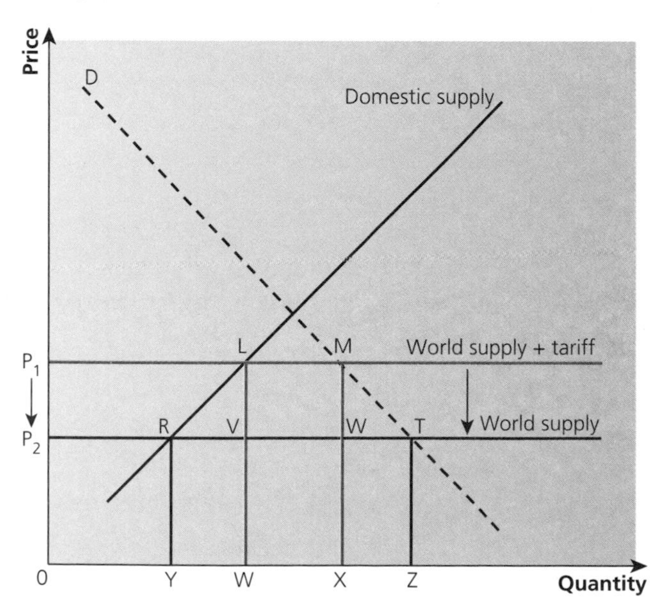

Figure 7.4 The effect of trade liberalisation

At the original price of P_1, domestic supply is 0W and imports are WX. After the tariff has been eliminated, the price falls to P_2, domestic supply falls to 0Y and imports rise to YZ.

- **Deregulation of capital markets:** this allows the flow of money between countries, so facilitating trade.
- **Promotion of foreign direct investment:** both of the above policies will help to contribute to an increase in foreign direct investment because TNCs will find it easier to trade.
- **Devaluation of exchange rates:** this would make exports more competitive, which would also give a boost to export-led growth.

This approach has been given added impetus by the collapse of communism, which led to increased integration of the Eastern bloc countries into the world economy. Further, countries, such as China and India, which have adopted these policies over the last 25 years, have enjoyed rapid rates of economic growth.

However, outward-looking strategies are not without problems:

- Countries may find that their **infant industries** are simply too small to be able to compete in world markets or with TNCs which establish themselves in the developing countries.
- TNCs may have a disruptive impact on the domestic economy.
- The financial crisis of 2008 demonstrated the dangers of close integration with the global economy in that problems quickly spread from one country to another.

Infant industries are newly established industries with small markets which are, therefore, too small to benefit from economies of scale.

Now test yourself Tested

6 How might inward-looking strategies be justified as a means of promoting development?

7 Give two reasons why trade liberalisation might help to promote development.

Answers on p. 112

Sectoral development: industrialisation

Revised

Industrialisation is often regarded as an essential characteristic of economic development.

Lewis's structural change (dual sector) model considers many developing countries at an early stage of development to have two sectors:

- A primarily agricultural economy, characterised by subsistence, low productivity and barter, with a large proportion of the population living in rural areas.
- A small modern industrial sector characterised by high productivity, monetary exchange and living in urban areas.

The Lewis model

Lewis's view is that economic development can only occur if there is industrialisation. This is illustrated in Figure 7.5.

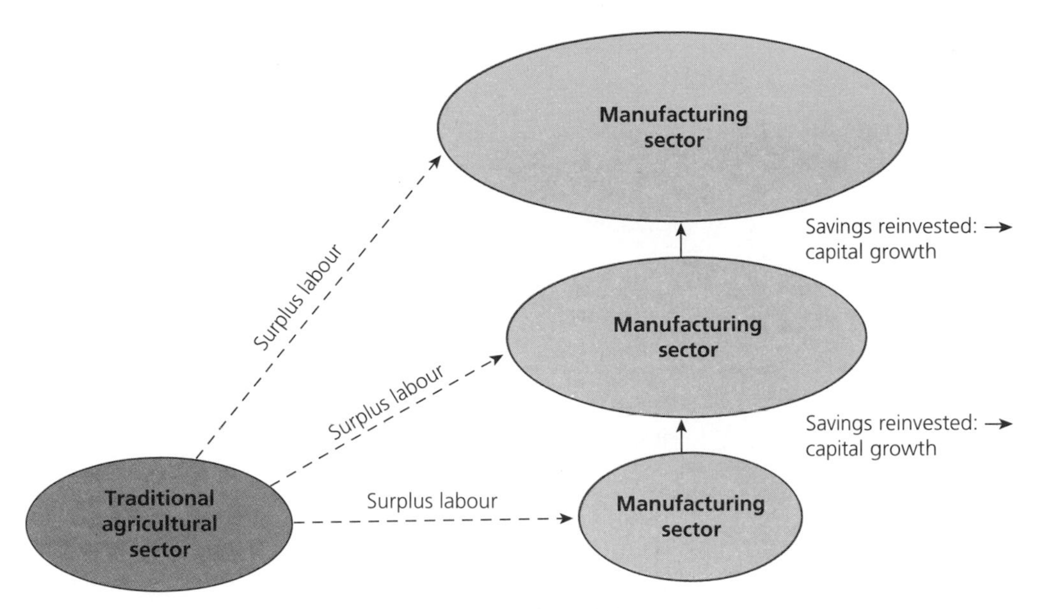

Figure 7.5 The Lewis structural change (dual sector) model

The key features of the Lewis model include:

- The transfer of surplus labour from the low-productivity agricultural sector to a higher-productivity industrial sector.
- Lewis thought that the **marginal productivity** of agricultural workers would be zero or close to zero because of the excess supply of workers. This analysis is based on the **law of diminishing returns**.
- Migration from the rural to urban areas was seen as desirable because the opportunity cost of the transfer of workers from the agricultural to the industrial sector would be zero or close to zero.
- Industrialisation requires investment, for example from TNCs, which will increase productivity and profitability. This model provides the rationale for government subsidies to attract investment from TNCs. Higher investment from TNCs should increase labour productivity which is likely to raise wages, so attracting workers from the rural areas.
- In turn, these companies may reinvest profits which should increase economic growth further.
- The share of profits and the savings ratio should increase as a proportion of GDP, so providing further funds for investment and continued economic growth.

Marginal productivity is the change in output resulting from the addition of one more unit of the variable factor.

The **law of diminishing** returns states that as successive units of a variable factor are added to fixed resources, the marginal product of the variable factor will eventually decline.

However, there are various criticisms of the Lewis model including:

- Profits made in the industrial sector might not be invested locally. For example, in the case of TNCs, profits may be repatriated to the foreign owners.
- Further investment might be in capital intensive production so that few new jobs are created.
- The assumption of surplus labour in the agricultural sector and full employment in the industrial sector is contradicted by the evidence. There is often widespread unemployment on the outskirts of large cities, e.g. the favelas in South America.
- Agriculture and primary products have formed the basis of growth and development in some countries.

Now test yourself

Tested

8 How might industrialisation affect the following:
   (a) The distribution of population between rural and urban areas.
   (b) The degree of inequality.
   (c) The environment.

Answers on p. 112

Sectoral development: tourism

Revised

Some countries have developed on the basis of investment in tourism, particularly when they have few raw materials. The expansion of tourism has strong attractions for a variety of reasons:

- **Source of foreign exchange:** tourists often spend significant sums of money on goods and services provided within the local economy. This helps to fill the foreign exchange gap and should help to improve the balance of payments on current account.
- **Investment by TNCs:** investment in hotels and associated services, for example, will have multiplier effects on GDP.
- **Infrastructure:** a focus on tourism will require investment in various forms of infrastructure including roads, airports, reservoirs, sewers and energy plants. Some of these may be provided by TNCs as part of agreements to allow them to build hotels. This investment will also have a multiplier effect on GDP. Therefore, there might be positive externalities for local businesses that benefit from the improved infrastructure.
- **Employment opportunities:** the tourist industry is **labour intensive** so the development of tourism should result in significant job creation.
- **Increased tax revenues:** all of the above factors should result in an increase in tax revenues for the government. These revenues may be used to reduce absolute poverty, improve public services and redistribute incomes.
- **Demand is income elastic:** this has the advantage that, when real incomes are rising, demand will increase more than proportionately.
- **Preservation of natural heritage:** the country has an incentive to preserve its natural heritage because this may be a key source of attraction to tourists.

Labour intensive industries are those which employ a high proportion of workers relative to capital.

However, there are various drawbacks to pursuing tourism as a means of development including:

- Adverse effect of the current account of the balance of payments — there are several reasons why tourism might cause a deterioration in the current account:
  - capital goods are required for the building of hotels and equipment is needed
  - food and gifts are demanded by tourists
  - profits may be repatriated to foreign shareholders of TNCs
- Fluctuations associated with the trade cycle — since demand for tourism is **income elastic**, then revenues from tourists might fall significantly during a recession.

Income elastic demand is when an increase in real income results in a more than proportionate increase in demand.

- External costs — tourists may cause an increase in waste, pollution of beaches and areas of outstanding beauty, destruction of ancient monuments, and water shortages for local people because priority is given to tourists.
- These external costs might cause some countries to impose restrictions on tourists — for example, the number of tourists to the Galapagos Islands is limited on a daily basis while visitors to Machu Picchu are limited by the requirement to have a guide.
- Changes in fashion — as with many other goods, tourism is subject to changes in tastes, preferences and fashions. Consequently, there is no long-term guarantee that a destination will always remain popular. Further, climate change might affect tourism. For example, if climate change results in less snow in some European ski resorts, numbers of tourists will inevitably decline in the winter months.
- Employment may be low paid and seasonal — typically, tourism is seasonal so workers might not have full-time, permanent jobs. In so far as the jobs created are relatively unskilled, it is likely that the wages will also be relatively low.
- Negative impact of cultural values — tourists might undermine the local way of life and destroy cultural values.

Now test yourself Tested

9 Why might foreign currency earnings from a developing country with a large tourist sector fluctuate?

Answers on p. 112

Sectoral development: agriculture and primary sector

Revised

As discussed above, economic development is usually associated with industrialisation. However, there are examples of countries who have achieved fast rates of growth and development as a result of developing their primary sectors, for instance Chile and Peru.

Chile has grown on the basis of its copper industry, and also of producing blueberries, papaya and wine. This approach to economic development may be appropriate if:

- The demand for the primary products being produced is income elastic.
- There is the potential for a large and growing demand for the particular primary product(s).
- There is the potential for large earnings of foreign currency.
- The country has a comparative advantage in the production of primary products. Such a comparative advantage should be viewed in a dynamic context: as the country experiences economic growth, the government may use the extra tax revenues being generated for education, which could give it a comparative advantage in other products in the future.
- The existence of primary products attracts FDI which could help to promote growth and development.

Examiner's tip

Economic development suggests that as a country becomes more developed, the proportion of workers employed in agriculture will decline while that employed in manufacturing and the tertiary (service) sectors increases. The most highly developed economies often have a high proportion of workers employed in the tertiary sector.

Aid

Revised

Aid refers to:

- the voluntary transfer of resources from one country to another; or
- to loans given on concessionary terms, i.e. at less than the market rate of interest

If aid is provided in the form of concessionary loans then there is a question as to whether conditions should be attached.

Official development assistance (ODA) relates specifically to aid provided by governments to developing countries and excludes aid provided by voluntary agencies.

Typical mistake

Confusion between aid and foreign direct investment (FDI). Whereas aid is a voluntary transfer of resources from one country to another, FDI is investment by a TNC in another country with the aim of making a profit.

The purpose of aid

- To reduce absolute poverty in the long run.
- To provide emergency relief following natural disasters such as floods, famines, earthquakes or other extreme weather events; or for refugees following a civil war. Essentially, this is short-term aid.

Types of aid

- **Tied aid:** this is aid with conditions attached. For example, there might be a requirement to buy goods from the donor country or the aid might be given in return for political and economic reforms.
- **Bilateral aid:** this is aid given directly by one country to another.
- **Multilateral aid:** this is aid provided by individual countries but channelled through organisations such as the World Bank to developing countries. To secure this aid, certain criteria usually have to be met.

UK's aid budget

In 2010, the UK government decided to ring-fence the overseas aid budget so that it would increase from £7.8 billion in 2010 to £11 billion by 2015. This was designed to meet the UN's target for developed countries to give 0.7% of GDP per year in foreign aid.

In 2011, Britain's total aid budget was £8.6 billion. Of this, around £3.6 billion was spent in the form of multilateral aid through the EU, the World Bank and the UN, and £5 billion was spent on bilateral aid, including debt relief and administration. Figure 7.6 shows the top ten recipients.

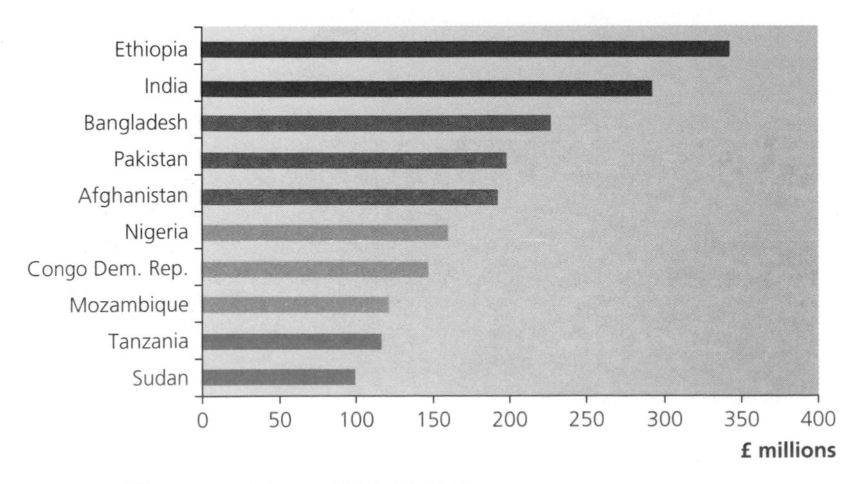

Figure 7.6 Top ten recipients of UK aid, 2011

The UK's commitment to increase aid may appear surprising given the cuts in government expenditure imposed on many other departments. The arguments for and against aid are outlined below.

The case for aid

There are a range of arguments for aid including:

- A reduction in absolute poverty — in turn, this should help to reduce child and maternal mortality.
- The reduction of inequality and relative poverty within a developing country.
- As a means of filling the savings gap — as explained earlier, the Harrod–Domar model illustrates the importance of savings for investment and economic growth.
- To provide funds for investment in infrastructure — these are essential if the country is to industrialise. Such investment is an injection into the circular flow of income and would, therefore, have a **multiplier** effect on GDP.
- To fill the foreign exchange gap — for example, the aid may be used to pay interest on debt owed to foreign countries or banks; or it might be used to finance the importation of capital goods.
- To improve human capital — through resources provided for education, healthcare, treatments towards HIV/AIDs, expertise in the training of teachers, doctors and healthcare workers.
- To promote entrepreneurship — which would help to establish new businesses and so lead to a higher rate of growth and development.

The **multiplier** describes the process whereby a change in an injection causes a proportionately larger change in GDP.

The case against aid

Despite the above advantages, many economists are sceptical about the value of aid to developing countries. Below are some of the arguments against aid:

- According to dependency theory, aid reinforces the dominance of developed economies over developing economies. This relationship stifles growth and development.
- There is a danger that a dependency culture will result. In other words, the recipients of aid become dependent on it and will not pursue appropriate macroeconomic policies to become independent.
- Aid funds fees to consultants; for example, the UK spent nearly £0.5 billion on firms working on third-world programmes. Many argue that this is not an efficient use of taxpayers' money.
- Aid is going to relatively rich countries. For example, in 2011, some of the £10 billion-a-year EU aid budget was channelled to countries such as Turkey, Iceland, Brazil and Barbados. Therefore, it is argued that aid frequently does not go to the neediest countries and people.
- Corruption means that aid might not reach those for whom it was intended. Instead, it may be diverted into military expenditure or expropriated by government officials for their own use.
- Inefficient allocation of resources: right-wing economists argue that aid distorts market forces and so will inevitably lead to a misallocation of resources.
- There may be political influence from the donor countries. Left-wing economists argue that aid is a form of imperialism whose primary aim is

to secure political influence over the countries to which aid is given. This may ultimately stifle growth and development in developing countries.

- Concessional loans involve an opportunity cost. Interest has to be paid on concessional loans, which means that the developing countries will have less money available for expenditure on health and education services.

Debt relief/cancellation

Revised

The heavy external debt burden on some of the poorest countries led to political pressure (for example, the Jubilee 2000 and Make Poverty History campaigns) to reduce or cancel their debts.

These debts are usually owed to all or to some of the following: the IMF, the World Bank, and governments and banks in developed countries.

The Heavily Indebted Poor Countries (HIPC) initiative

- The HIPC initiative was started in 1996 by the International Monetary Fund (IMF) and World Bank with the aim of reducing the external debt of the poorest countries of the world to sustainable levels.
- Changes were made in 1999 to make the process quicker and also to strengthen the links between debt relief, poverty reduction and social policies.
- In 2005, the HIPC was enhanced by the Multilateral Debt Relief Initiative (MDRI) in order to speed up the process of meeting the Millennium Development Goals, for example, halving absolute poverty by 2015.
- By 2012, 36 countries had approval for debt-reduction packages under the HIPC initiative.
- 30 countries were in Africa, accounting for $76 billion in debt-service relief. Three additional countries are eligible for assistance from the HIPC initiative.

Arguments for debt cancellation

- **It helps to reduce absolute poverty:** more money and resources are available for those unable to meet their basic needs.
- **It helps to reduce the foreign exchange gap:** without the obligation to pay interest on the debt or, indeed, the capital, developing countries have more foreign currency available to purchase imported capital goods.
- **It helps to reduce the savings gap:** following debt cancellation, developing countries have more funds available for investment in infrastructure and for expenditure on developing human capital.
- **Increased confidence:** debt relief or complete cancellation might increase business confidence in the prospects for the country's economy. In turn, this might lead to an increase in domestic investment and in foreign direct investment.
- **Environmental gains:** conditions might be attached to the cancellation of debts. For example, the developing country might have to agree to take measures to improve and protect the environment. These are called 'debt-for-nature swaps'.
- **Mutual benefits:** if debt cancellation results in increased growth, then developing countries might be able to buy more goods from developed countries in the future so benefiting their economies.

Arguments against debt cancellation

- **Time:** it takes a considerable time to agree a debt cancellation programme whereas an aid programme is likely to be implemented more quickly.
- **Moral hazard problem:** there is the possibility that the country whose debts have been cancelled may pursue unsound macroeconomic policies and run up further debts in the future.
- **Corruption:** if there is significant corruption among government officials, then the money saved may be wasted.
- **Impact on financial institutions in developed countries:** banks and their shareholders may bear some of the burden of debt cancellation. This may make them less willing to lend to developing countries in the future.
- **HIPC scheme does not help all those in poverty:** large numbers of poor people live in countries with relatively low levels of debt but these would not be helped by the HIPC scheme.

The **moral hazard problem** occurs when the person/firm/country taking the risk may not be the one who bears the consequences of that risk.

As with aid, there is an argument that other measures might be much more effective in securing growth and development. In particular, the removal of trade barriers by developed countries is often cited as a key measure because it would open markets for the goods from developing countries.

Typical mistake

Misunderstanding of debt. In this context, the debt referred to is external debt, i.e. owed to foreigners.

Now test yourself Tested ☐

10 What is the difference between aid and foreign direct investment?

11 How does debt contribute to the foreign currency gap?

Answers on p. 112

Microfinance

Revised ☐

This is a means of providing extremely poor people with small loans (microcredit) to help them engage in productive activities or to grow their tiny businesses. The pioneer of microfinance was Mohammed Yunus, who established the Grameen Bank in Bangladesh.

Another key player in this area was Vikram Akula who was the founder and former chairperson of SKS Microfinance, an organisation that offers microloans and insurance to poor women in impoverished areas of India.

Key characteristics of microfinance schemes

- They aim to lend to those who would have no access to sources of finance from the formal sector and who would, therefore, be forced to pay very high rates of interest.
- Entrepreneurs mutually guarantee each other's loans forming a community bank.
- Loans can be as little as £25 enabling clients to buy basic equipment, e.g. a sewing machine, seed or fertiliser.
- Profits can be used to buy more stock or seed or to start a new business.
- Microcredit must be repaid. In practice, 97% of loans are repaid.
- Interest is charged to cover the costs incurred.

The main clients of microfinance

- Women, who form more than 97% of clients.
- The self-employed, often household-based entrepreneurs.
- Small farmers in rural areas.
- Small shopkeepers, street vendors and service providers in urban areas.

Criticisms of microfinance

- It is based on the premise that poor people can make themselves richer if they are provided with access to credit. In practice, wealth creation depends on the skills and knowledge of institutions as well as individuals.
- Microfinance is not self-financing unless there is assistance from the government or from aid agencies.
- High interest rates are charged without outside assistance.
- Most loans are not used to start up businesses but to fund extraordinary items of expenditure.
- Microfinance is not very successful at creating prosperous small businesses in the long run.
- An overemphasis on microfinance might lead to a reduction in aid.

Recently, the emphasis in this area has shifted to the concept of 'financial inclusion', which relates to how people save, borrow, make payments and manage risk. In other words, it is concerned with, for example, access to banks and other financial institutions.

Fair-trade schemes

Revised

The aims of fair-trade schemes are as follows:

- The primary aim is 'to address the injustice of low prices' by guaranteeing that producers receive a fair price.
- This means paying producers a price above the free-market level for their produce, provided that they meet particular labour and production standards.

The market for fair-trade products has grown rapidly and there are now over 3000 product lines including coffee, tea, chocolate, bananas, wines, flowers and clothes.

Advantages of fair-trade schemes:

These schemes enjoy wide public support in the UK which is reflected in the growth of sales of these products. Indeed, some towns have been designated as 'fair-trade towns' if they meet certain criteria set out by the Fairtrade Foundation. The appeal of fair trade arises from the following:

- Producers receive a fair price for their products (higher than the market price).
- Extra money is available to spend on education, health, infrastructure, clean water supplies, conversion to organic farming and other development programmes.
- Producers are shielded from wildly fluctuating prices, which enables them to plan investment and output.
- Higher prices result in higher revenues which producers can use to improve the quality of products.
- Producers may be encouraged to diversify into other products.

Criticisms of fair-trade schemes

- The amount of the extra money spent by consumers which is available to spend on social projects is exaggerated and may be close to zero.
- Some poorer or remote farmers cannot organise and join up to the scheme while others cannot afford the fees and still others will be working for larger producers who are excluded from many fair-trade product lines.
- Distortion of market forces: the artificial high prices encourage existing producers to increase output and new producers to enter the market. If market forces were left to operate, then the low prices would be a signal to producers to switch production to alternative crops.
- Guaranteeing a minimum price does not provide an incentive for producers to improve the quality of the product.
- Certification of Fairtrade is based on normative views on the best way to organise labour. For example, in the case of coffee, certification is only available to cooperatives of small producers.
- It might provide a dependency trap for producers, i.e. they become dependent on the money received from the scheme.
- Consumers in developed countries pay higher prices for Fairtrade products. However, it is argued that a high proportion of the higher price goes to the profits of the retailers rather than to the producer.

Examiner's tip

All methods of promoting economic development should be considered critically. Remember that evaluative skills are very important.

International financial institutions

The International Monetary Fund (IMF)

Revised

The IMF was founded in 1944 with the objective of avoiding the policies which led to the Depression of the 1930s by increasing international liquidity and providing stability in capital markets through a system of convertible currencies pegged to the dollar. It also lent to countries with temporary balance of payments deficits on current account.

Membership and finance

There are now 188 members of the IMF.

When a country joins, it is required to pay a quota which is broadly based on its relative size in the world economy (calculated in terms of its GDP). Up to 25% of this quota or subscription must be paid in the Special Drawing Rights or currencies which are generally acceptable such as the US dollar, the pound sterling, yen or the euro. The quota is important because it determines:

- voting rights and
- the amount which may be borrowed from the IMF

Impact of the 2008 global financial crisis

The role of the IMF changed significantly following the crisis:

- **Increased lending:** the IMF responded quickly to the global economic crisis, with lending commitments reaching a record level of more than US $250 billion in 2010.

- **More flexibility in lending:** the IMF changed its way of operation so that it is better able to respond to the individual needs of countries.
- **Providing forecasts, analysis and advice:** the IMF's monitoring, forecasts, and policy advice, informed by a global perspective and by experience from previous crises, have been in high demand and have been used by the G20.
- **Developing future policy:** the IMF is considering the implications of the crisis for policy and regulation.

Special Drawing Rights

In 2009, the G20 summit authorised the IMF to issue $250 billion in new Special Drawing Rights (SDRs). An SDR is sometimes referred to as the IMF's currency but it is, in fact, the IMF's unit of account. The value of an SDR is defined as the value of a fixed amount of yen, dollars, pounds and euros, expressed in dollars at the current exchange rate. These SDRs represent a potential claim on other countries' foreign currency reserves, for which they can be exchanged voluntarily. On the other hand, countries with high foreign currency reserves can buy SDRs from countries that need hard currency.

The IBRD/World Bank

Revised

The original role of the International Bank for Reconstruction and Development (IBRD)/World Bank was to provide long-term loans for reconstruction and development to member nations who suffered in the Second World War.

In the 1970s, its role changed to setting up agricultural reforms in developing countries, giving loans and providing expertise.

Structural Adjustment Programmes (SAPs)

- In 1982, Mexico defaulted on its loan repayments. As a result the World Bank now imposes Structural Adjustment Programmes which set out conditions on which loans are given. The aim is to ensure that debtor countries do not default on the repayment of debts.
- SAPs were based on free-market reforms (e.g. trade liberalisation, removal of state subsidies on food, privatisation and reduction in public expenditure to reduce budget deficits). However, these free-market reforms have been criticised because they:
  - did little to help the world's poor
  - failed to promote development
  - increased inequality
  - caused environmental degradation
  - resulted in social and political chaos in many countries

Poverty reduction strategies

There was widespread criticism of SAPs and the devastating effect which they had on some developing countries. Consequently, the World Bank now focuses on poverty reduction strategies, with aid being directed towards:

- countries following sound macroeconomic policies
- healthcare and broadening education
- local communities rather than central governments

The future of the IMF and World Bank

Now the roles of the IMF and the World Bank have become blurred: both have a role in the developing world and in poverty reduction and it is suggested that they should be reformed to reflect the changing needs of the global economy. For example:

- The **IMF** should be slimmed down and should undertake short-term lending to crisis-hit countries.
- The **World Bank** should act as a development agency and undertake a detailed credit appraisal of the creditworthiness of recipient countries.

Non-government organisations (NGOs)

Revised

The work of NGOs has brought **community-based development** to the forefront of strategies to promote growth and development (i.e. the focus has moved away from state-managed schemes). The key characteristics of these community-based schemes are:

- local control of small-scale projects
- self-reliance
- emphasis on using the skills available
- environmental sustainability

Exam practice

Essay questions

1 **(a)** Assess the view that primary product dependency is a constraint on economic growth and development in developing countries. [20]

(b) Evaluate ways in which economic growth and development might be promoted in developing countries. [30]

2 **(a)** Assess the significance of factors which might limit growth in developing countries. [20]

(b) Evaluate aid and trade liberalisation as methods of promoting economic development in developing countries. [30]

Data-response question

Extract: Sub-Saharan Africa

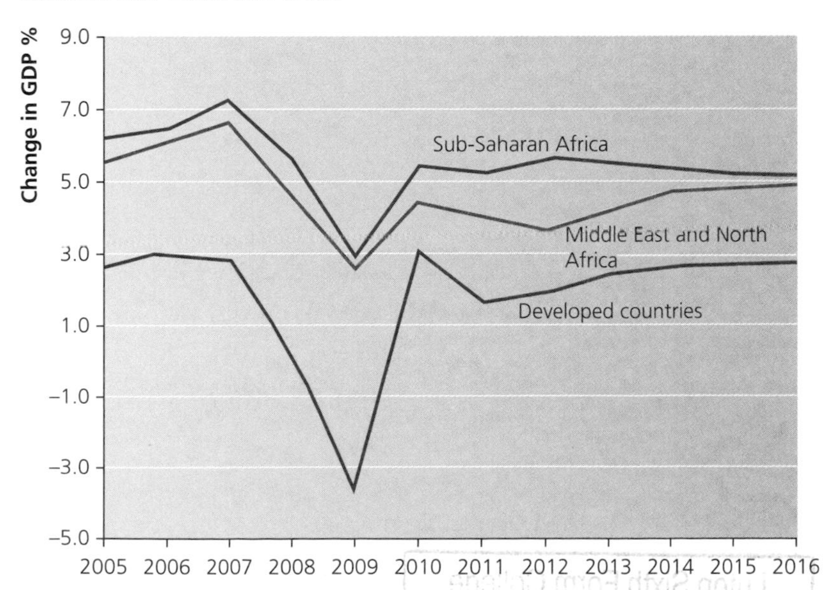

Figure 7.7 Sub-Saharan Africa and the global economy — GDP percentage change on previous years

Figure 7.7 shows that, although the economies of Sub-Saharan countries suffered a fall in their growth rates following the financial crisis, the economies of developed countries were affected much more severely. The banks and stock exchanges of Sub-Saharan countries were not well-integrated into the global economy and foreign direct investment remained fairly steady.

Although most of these economies avoided recessions, their growth rates slowed. Combined with their rapid population growth rates, this caused a fall in average living standards. For example, in 2010 Kenya's growth rate fell to around 3%. However, average growth rates are expected to be around or above 5% from 2012 to 2016, not least because foreign direct investment is expected to increase as countries such as China continue to invest in the primary sectors of these countries.

Sub-Saharan countries are also increasing their trade with emerging economies such as Russia and China. The reason is that these countries are importing raw materials such as oil, cotton, iron ore and copper from the Sub-Saharan African countries. However, some development economists think that the path to development lies in industrialisation whereas this growth in trade would make them more dependent on primary products.

3 **(a)** Explain why, despite positive growth rates, some Sub-Saharan African countries faced 'a fall in average living standards'. [5]

(b) With reference to the information provided, analyse why the growth rate of the Sub-Saharan African economies was higher than that of advanced economies between 2009 and 2011. [8]

(c) With reference to the information provided and your own knowledge, assess the benefits to African countries of increased trade with emerging economies. [10]

(d) Assess the case for an increase in aid to countries in Sub-Saharan Africa. [12]

(e) To what extent do the benefits of foreign direct investment in the primary sector industries of countries in Sub-Saharan Africa outweigh the costs? [15]

Answers and quick quizzes online

Online

Examiner's summary

You should have an understanding of:

- ✔ Factors which constrain growth and development including:
  - primary product dependency
  - savings gap and foreign exchange gap
  - debt; population issues
- ✔ Ways of promoting growth and development including:
  - state interventionist approaches
  - free-market approaches.
  - inward-looking strategies
  - outward-looking strategies
  - aid; debt relief
  - microfinance; fair-trade schemes
- ✔ International financial institutions: the IMF; the World Bank; and non-government organisations.

Now test yourself answers

Chapter 1

1 Yes and yes: profit maximisation is a balanced point which rational firms try to achieve unless the question tells you otherwise.

2 It is revenue maximising, which is rational because the costs become irrelevant when the stock has to be thrown away. The seller should make as much money as possible, ignoring the marginal cost.

3 Lower, if the demand curve is sloping downwards. The firm needs to lower the price to sell more, and as it does so the marginal profit is negative — that is it costs more to make each extra unit than is received from selling the extra unit.

4 The firms might have other objectives apart from short-run profit maximisation. If the owners can be kept happy with a certain amount of profit then other goals can be worked on.

5 The main benefits are those of horizontal integration, i.e. economies of scale and increased market share. However there are also advantages in bailing out a firm that might have been about to become insolvent.

6 The company is niche market, with a low minimum efficient scale. The cars are worth more to consumers partly because they are so rare!

7 You should raise the price. Total revenue will rise, by definition.

8 It depends on the type of business as to how much money is needed to keep factors in their current use.

9 Normal profit is built into the cost curve. So if AC = AR or TC = TR you know that the firm is operating at normal profit.

10 It depends on the type of workers. If your workers are paid relative to the amount they produce, for example strawberry pickers, then they are variable costs. But if they are paid whether or not you produce anything, such as health and safety officers, they are fixed costs.

11 The law of diminishing returns sets in.

12 Yes. When the marginal product falls, it means that there is a smaller increase in output when one more factor is employed — that is, it means that the law of diminishing returns has set in.

13 8, that is $2 \times 2 \times 2$. That's quite a big increase after doubling the lengths.

14 It should decrease output, which means the long-run average costs will fall.

15 Internal economies occur when the firm gets larger, and external economies occur when the industry gets larger.

16 Yes. If the demand and MR curves both pass through the lowest point of the AC curve then P = MC and MC = AC. This only happens in the long run in perfect competition.

17 Profit is maximised.

18 No. In fact a firm could be the only firm in the market (monopoly) but have no barriers to entry. But it is unlikely to be making a profit, or other firms would enter.

Chapter 2

1 Because they are covering AVC and making a contribution to the fixed costs. If all costs are variable, the firm will leave the industry, which is what happens in the long run as there are no fixed costs in the long run.

2 Monopolies can make prices higher and restrict choice for consumers, amongst other costs.

3 If there were no monopoly power, new firms could enter the industry and exploit the supernormal profits that are available when a price discriminator charges a higher price to the consumer with a lower price elasticity of demand.

4 Monopoly power means that a firm has power over consumers, and monopsony means a firm has power over suppliers.

5 Legally they can both be treated as monopolies. However the fact that the two-firm concentration ratio appears to be 52% means this also meets the rule for oligopoly. In this case we would call the market structure a duopoly because two firms are in control of the market.

6 It is overt collusion because it is openly asking a question about future prices. However it is not guaranteed that the firms will act on the information and it might be very hard to detect this.

7 Nothing for revenue. Both raising and lowering price causes revenue to fall. To raise profits the firm needs to cut its costs or diversify into new markets. Or it could collude with other firms.

8 Contestability brings the benefits of competition or removes some of the problems of monopolies without other firms actually having to enter the market.

Chapter 3

1 Competition can lead to lower prices and more choice for consumers.

2 Competition policy is used to promote competition within markets, and to remove any factors that significantly lessen competition. Regulation is used to control firms where competition alone cannot create the best conditions for efficiency in markets.

3 The annual cost of leasing the projects does appear, but there are no up-front costs for the capital expenditure.

Chapter 4

1
- Change from inward-looking strategy to outward-looking strategy, leading to foreign direct investment (FDI).
- FDI combined with low labour costs leading to development of manufacturing industries and increased exports.
- Rising real incomes in emerging and developing economies creating extra demand for goods produced in China.

2 Absolute advantage implies that one country can produce more of a product than another country. Comparative advantage means that a country can produce a product at a lower opportunity cost than another country. So even if country A can produce more of all products than country B, specialisation and trade will still be beneficial if B has a relative or comparative advantage in one of the products.

3 Advantages: more choice; lower prices and, therefore, increased consumers' surplus.

Disadvantages: consumers may face less choice in the long run if domestic firms are unable to compete and so go bankrupt. In turn, this might imply that workers in the domestic industries are made redundant.

4 Advantages: lower cost of imported raw materials; larger market for the goods produced which might enable firms to benefit from economies of scale. Both these factors might enable firms to increase profits.

Disadvantages: inability to compete with foreign competitors; lower profits and the possibility that firms might go bankrupt.

5
- Tariffs bring in tax revenue for the government whereas a subsidy will cause an increase in government expenditure.
- Tariffs cause a rise in the price of goods whereas subsidies to domestic firms will not.

6 The primary aim of the WTO is to promote free trade and the theoretical basis for free trade is the law of comparative advantage.

7 These terms are usually applied when considering trading blocs and protectionist policies. Trade creation relates to increased trade with other countries following the removal of trade barriers. Trade diversion occurs when trade barriers are imposed. This usually causes trade flows to be diverted from low cost producers to high cost producers.

8 Reasons include:
- Continued fall in protectionist measures as more countries join trading blocs and WTO negotiates lower trade barriers.
- Further specialisation by countries based on the law of comparative advantage.
- Growth of emerging economies that will both export more and import more, as real incomes increase.

9 Firms can access world markets more easily by advertising on the internet. It is easier for consumers to buy goods from other countries. Both these factors contribute to the growth of trade and globalisation.

Chapter 5

1 **(a)** Visible export: inflow into the trade in goods balance which is part of the current account. Positive effect on the current account of the balance of payments.

(b) Invisible import: outflow from the trade in services balance which is part of the current account. Negative effect on the current account of the balance of payments.

(c) Inflow into the financial account. Positive effect on the financial account of the balance of payments.

(d) Visible import: outflow from the trade in goods balance which is part of the current account. Negative effect on the current account of the balance of payments.

(e) Outflow from the current account under the 'investment income' balance. Negative effect on the current account of the balance of payments.

2 **(a)** An improvement, because these countries will have more money to spend on UK exports.

(b) A deterioration, because this will make the UK's goods less competitive and so less attractive to other countries, causing a fall in UK exports and an increase in imports.

(c) A deterioration, because this will make the UK's goods less competitive since average costs and prices of UK goods will increase.

(d) An improvement, because UK consumers will have less disposable income causing a fall in imports.

3 Demand-side policies relate to those which affect aggregate demand. Either fiscal or monetary policy may be used.

Fiscal policy: to reduce a current account deficit, public expenditure could be reduced or taxes increased. Both of these would reduce aggregate demand within the country and so cause a fall in consumption and a fall in imports.

Monetary policy: an increase in interest rates would increase the incentive to save. In contrast there would be less incentive to borrow because a higher rate of interest would be payable on loans. Again the overall effect would be to decrease imports.

However, it should be noted that an increase in interest rates could cause an increase in the value of the country's currency which would cause a fall in the competitiveness of its goods (because the foreign currency price of exports would increase and the price of imports would decrease).

4 **(a)** Yes, because inward investment causes an increase in demand for US dollars.

(b) No, because the purchasing power of the dollar would be falling relative to other countries' currencies.

(c) No, because money is likely to flow out of the USA to foreign banks where the interest rates are higher.

(d) Yes, because this is likely to increase the demand for dollars by foreigners.

5 Effects include:
- Fall in competitiveness of the country's goods.
- This could cause a deterioration in the current account of the balance of payments.
- If the country's goods are less competitive then unemployment may increase and real output may fall.
- The fall in the price of imported raw materials will help to reduce cost–push inflationary pressures.
- Possibility of an increase in living standards because less has to be exported to gain a given quantity of imports — the terms of trade will have risen.

6 **(a)** Increase competitiveness.

(b) Increase competitiveness because the costs of firms would be reduced.

(c) Decrease competitiveness because wage costs would rise causing an overall increase in the costs of production, which is likely to lead to an increase in prices.

(d) Increase competitiveness because new technology is likely to result in an increase in productivity.

(e) Increase competitiveness because a better skilled workforce is likely to be more productive.

Chapter 6

1 The most important reason is the ageing population, which means increased expenditure on pensions and other benefits for the elderly.

2
- Health care because of an ageing population. The elderly tend to make much greater demands on the NHS.
- Debt interest because the size of the national debt is increasing and so interest payments are likely to increase significantly.
- Aid budget because the government is committed to increasing aid so that it is 0.7% of GDP.

3 Disincentive effects may mean that workers withdraw from the workforce, do less overtime, or may move to another country (tax exiles). The Laffer curve may be used to illustrate the effects of changes in tax rates on tax revenues.

4 If demand is price elastic above a particular price then an increase in tax would result in a fall in tax revenue. Remember that price elasticity of demand varies along a straight line demand schedule.

5 A budget deficit is the excess of public expenditure over tax revenue in a particular year whereas the national debt is the cumulative total of past government borrowing.

6
- If the deficit is being used to fund long-term capital projects which are designed to increase long-run aggregate supply.
- If the deficit is cyclical and, therefore, temporary, associated with a slowdown in the economy.
- Another reason is more contentious, based on a Keynesian approach, i.e. to stimulate the economy in time of recession.

7 With an increasing national debt, there will be an increase in the amount of interest which has to be paid servicing it. Therefore, the opportunity cost may be new hospitals or schools. These would have to be sacrificed to pay the interest.

8
- In the economic circumstances of 2011–12 with interest rates at historically low levels and virtually stagnant economic growth, monetary policy has little impact because: there is little scope for further reductions in interest rates and, following the financial crisis, banks are risk averse and are unwilling to lend.
- Businesses and consumers may lack confidence in the future of the economy and so may be unwilling to take on new debt

9 **(a)** This should reduce the fiscal deficit immediately because government expenditure should fall. Further, if it encourages the unemployed to take jobs, then tax revenue should increase. However, if the only effect is a fall in aggregate demand, the fiscal deficit will increase.

(b) At first sight, it may be thought that there would be an increase in the budget deficit because government expenditure will increase. However, if it results in a significant increase in the number of women in employment then tax revenues would increase.

(c) Again, it might be thought that this would cause a fall in tax revenues so causing an increase in the fiscal deficit. However, if this results in an increase in domestic and foreign direct investment, then this could result in an increase in tax revenues so reducing the fiscal deficit in the longer term.

10 No. It is possible for there to be significant falls in absolute poverty while relative poverty is increasing. Remember that relative poverty involves making a comparison with others in that country so even if a country has a very high GDP per head, there will always be people in relative poverty and that level could be increasing.

11
- Inheritance: money and inherited assets are a major source of inequality.
- Ownership of assets, e.g. property: those owning property have enjoyed substantial increases in their wealth in most countries over the last 50 years.

12 The Lorenz curve would move further away from the 45° line.

Chapter 7

1 Supply and demand are very price inelastic so any shift in either the supply or demand curve would cause a significant price change. The following diagram shows how changes in growing conditions have caused shifts in the supply curve and, consequently in the price.

- The initial equilibrium price in Year 1 is P_1.
- If there is a good harvest in Year 2, the price will fall to P_2.
- Following a bad harvest in year 3, the price will rise to P_3.

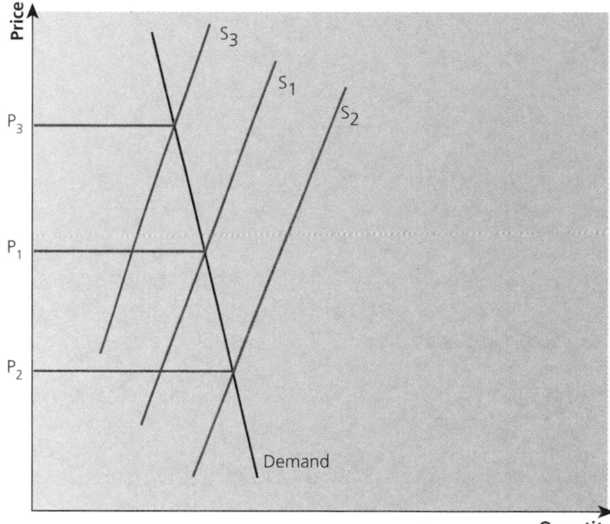

2

(a) Terms of trade $= \dfrac{\text{index of export prices}}{\text{index of import prices}} \times 100$

$= \dfrac{104}{112} \times 100$

$= 92.86$

(b) The terms of trade have decreased which implies that more must be exported to gain a given quantity of imports. In turn, this suggests that living standards have fallen. However, the fall in the terms of trade indicates that the country's goods are more competitive, which could result in an improvement in its balance of payments which could lead to an increase in growth.

3 With low incomes, the marginal propensity to consume would be high because people would tend to spend much of their income and any increase in income. Consequently, savings would be low so that funds for investment would be limited.

4 A shortage of foreign exchange would mean that there would be insufficient funds for importing capital goods or essential raw materials and oil or health care products. In turn, it may be difficult for the country to achieve economic growth and generate tax revenues which could be used to improve education (and literacy rates); healthcare (and life expectancy); and improvements in access to clean water etc.

5 If population is growing at a faster rate than the growth in real GDP, then GDP per head will fall.

6 In the early stages of development, a country may require protectionist measures to enable its infant industries to become established and gain sufficient economies of scale to be efficient enough to compete on world markets.

7
- If an economy is open to trade, it is more likely that transnational companies will invest in the country. This will generate economic growth and, with higher real incomes, development might occur, e.g. in terms of improved education and healthcare.
- Removal of trade barriers will act as an incentive for domestic firms to become more efficient and productive. With higher growth, economic development is more likely.

8 **(a)** Industrialisation is usually associated with increased urbanisation as manufacturing firms cluster in certain places and towns grow up around them.

(b) In the early stages of industrialisation, inequality usually increases. Various reasons may be used to explain this. For example, the Lewis model suggests that workers in manufacturing industries will be more productive than agricultural workers. Further, TNCs are likely to pay higher wages than workers would earn in the country's agricultural sector.

(c) Again, in the early stages of industrialisation, there are usually considerable negative externalities such as pollution from factories; damage to the rural environment caused by the building of factories, roads and houses; and water pollution.

9 There are several possible reasons:
- Demand for tourism is critically dependent on the state of the world economy because demand is income elastic.
- Many developing countries dependent on tourism are subject to extreme weather events such as hurricanes.
- Obviously, demand for tourism in some countries may be seasonal so foreign currency earnings fluctuate between seasons.

10 Aid is the free transfer of resources from one country to another. FDI is investment by a TNC in another country whose shareholders expect to make a profit from the investment.

11 To service the debt, i.e. to make interest payments on the debt, the country will have to pay in foreign currency, meaning that there is less available for purchasing capital goods, oil, food etc.